W9-BLE-748

THE BOOK
THAT CHANGED
MY LIFE

THE NATIONAL
BOOK FOUNDATION

THE BOOK
THAT CHANGED
MY LIFE

INTERVIEWS WITH NATIONAL BOOK AWARD
WINNERS AND FINALISTS

Edited by Diane Osen

Introduction by Neil Baldwin

THE MODERN LIBRARY

NEW YORK

2002 Modern Library Paperback Edition

Copyright © 2002 by the National Book Foundation
Introduction copyright © 2002 by Neil Baldwin

All rights reserved under International and Pan-American Copyright
Conventions. Published in the United States by Modern Library, a division of
Random House, Inc., New York, and simultaneously in Canada by Random
House of Canada Limited, Toronto.

MODERN LIBRARY and the TORCHBEARER Design are registered trademarks
of Random House, Inc.

LIBRARY OF CONGRESS CATALOGING-IN-PUBLICATION DATA

The book that changed my life: interviews with National Book Award winners
and finalists/edited by Diane Osen; introduction by Neil Baldwin.—2002
Modern Library pbk. ed.
p. cm.
ISBN 0-679-78351-2
1. Authors, American—20th century—Books and reading.   2. Authors,
American—20th century—Interviews.   3. Authorship.   I. Osen, Diane, 1956-

Z1039.A87 B66 2002
810.9'0054—dc21   2002141583

Modern Library website address: www.modernlibrary.com

Printed in the United States of America

2 4 6 8 9 7 5 3 1

To my Beloved Parents

ACKNOWLEDGMENTS

I owe a great deal to a great many. First and foremost, I wish to thank Neil Baldwin, executive director of the National Book Foundation, for his illuminating introduction to this book, for his enthusiastic support of the project, and for his enduring friendship. I am profoundly grateful as well to Meredith Andrews, Maryann Jacob, and Sherrie Young—the program officers of the National Book Foundation—for five years of expert advice and cheerful assistance; and to Meg Kearney, associate director of the Foundation, for many insightful suggestions.

I am indebted, too, to the remarkable writers who donated so much time and effort to this project; they and their books have changed my life beyond measure. Thank you all: James Carroll, Don DeLillo, E. L. Doctorow, Charles Johnson, Diane Johnson, Philip Levine, David Levering Lewis, Barry Lopez, David McCullough, Alice McDermott, Cynthia Ozick, Grace Paley, Linda Pastan, Katherine Paterson, and Robert Stone.

Many thanks as well to Peter Olson, chairman of Random House, for not only acquiring *The Book That Changed My Life*, but for overseeing the generous donation of all profits from the book to the National Book Foundation; to Ann Godoff, publisher of Random House, for ensuring that the book found just the right home within the house; and to David Ebershoff, publishing director of the Modern Library, for laboring so skillfully and lovingly over the manuscript.

Finally, I thank my husband, Rick, and my daughter Serena, with all my heart.

Contents

INTRODUCTION

Neil Baldwin

"Do not all the achievements of a poet's predecessors and contemporaries rightly belong to him? Why should he shrink from picking flowers where he finds them? Only by making the riches of the others our own do we bring anything great into being."

—JOHANN WOLFGANG VON GOETHE

"I want to point to the elected presences which makers construe within themselves or within their works, to the 'fellow-travellers,' teachers, critics, dialectical partners, to those other voices within their own which can give even the most complexly solitary and innovative of creative acts a shared, collective fabric."

—GEORGE STEINER, *Grammars of Creation*

Allow me to introduce the person who invented the provocative, multifaceted conceit for *The Book That Changed My Life,* the book you hold in your hands, the book that may very well change *your* life, as it has mine.

I have known and worked closely with Diane Osen, the editor of this volume, since a mild, late-spring day in 1989, when she came to my office at the New York Public Library to congratulate me for taking on the daunting challenge of executive director of the brand-new National Book Foundation. As public-relations counsel to the fledgling organization, she had been sent as a welcoming emissary on behalf of a group of board members led by Chairman Al Silverman. I was instantly charmed by this bright-eyed, dark-haired, smiling, well-spoken, professionally put-together, and unflaggingly upbeat young woman who had read all of Trollope. We went on to brainstorm and work together on a succession of literary and educational projects over the ensuing decade and more—sophisticated, image-building PR, Diane's earlier forte, was merely the beginning of our collaboration—and I came to appreciate and respect her passion for books and reading.

I would prefer obsession (in the good sense) to passion, because this is the second compendium of National Book Award essays and interviews published bearing Diane's byline. The first compilation, likewise brought out as a philanthropic gesture by Random House, was *The Writing Life* in 1995. Reflecting upon the dozens of long conversations and reams of correspondence she has conducted with contemporary authors, Diane told me recently that she is trying to "share with the reader" the same thrill of immediacy she experiences, the awareness of how privileged and fortunate she is to be in a position to chat so openly with such a broad spectrum of admired writers.

Her methodology is rigorous. She prepares by reading everything she can about and by the author. Then, in keeping with the unique theme of the current volume, she becomes familiar with the literary works, as she expresses it, that have shaped the subject's writing life, in many cases since childhood. She prepares a roster of carefully worded questions before picking up the telephone at the appointed time for the conversation, and she always advises her subject that she does indeed have questions at hand. Once the interview tape gets rolling, more often than not Diane intuitively modifies her direction when moods shift and attentions diverge, but as you will soon pleasurably discover, freshness and spontaneity are preserved.

What is the overarching message she is trying to convey, the largest lesson she has learned? I asked the intrepid editor. Without hesitating, as if the answer were engraved on her psyche, Diane replied, "Stories are essential to our very nature as human beings."

Even before Diane came up with the informing concept for this book, I had been turning over and over in my own mind the mutating meanings of "influence," a tricky word when applied to the process of making literature. Unlike small tributaries flowing reliably, by natural force of gravity, into the larger river, influences are often not discernible to the person who is asked to identify and then attribute significance to them, within himself or in others. Can an influence have an effect upon us if we have forgotten it? How do we quantify its power? If a literary critic points to an influence upon a writer's work, does it matter if the writer—or reader—accepts the theory or not?

This intrusive dilemma ambushed me while I was watching Kate Burton present an incendiary Hedda Gabler, managing to take over every corner of the stage simultaneously, infecting all the other characters—husband, ex-lover, friend—with her desperate passions. A chain of intellectual free associations that are the curse of the overeducated pushed their way to the surface of my brain while I struggled to keep my appreciation focused upon the performance itself: Ibsen...naturalism...James Joyce...some essay or review he wrote about the playwright...oh yes, then there was Joyce's own play, *The Dead*...but it wasn't just about a style of stage drama with Joyce, it was also the "modern" psychological drama at work in the unconscious...you mean Stephen Dedalus's journey to maturity? (I asked myself, inventorying my dusty undergraduate reading list)...no, more appropriately, Leopold Bloom's thoughts...the counterpoint of his perambulating inner drama played out against what was "actually" happening on June 16, 1904...yes, but remember, *Ulysses* was a work of fiction, so it wasn't *really* happening in Dublin, in the strictest sense...enough of this meandering...back to the play on stage. Good grief, she is burning the manuscript!

Another Bloom—the critic, Harold—cast a long shadow on this elusive topic with his 1973 classic, *The Anxiety of Influence*. I was quite taken then by his thesis that the artist, "irresistibly" compelled to look back in trepidation, is condemned to appropriate the ideas of his predecessors within the intimate, solitary labor of his own creation. This unavoidable retrospective act, intrinsic to all art, brings along with it a "matrix of relationships," defensive misreadings, and compositional problems, giving the lie to the cherished ideal known as originality.

I have trouble, now, three decades later, assimilating Bloom's severe and "daemonic" vision of influence when I turn to the evocative recollections of childhood and youth and memorable books expressed by the fifteen authors in *The Book That Changed My Life*, be it James Carroll leaving the seminary, and then reading Camus; Don DeLillo playing street games, and reading Hart Crane; E. L. Doctorow talking to his grandfather, and reading *Robinson Crusoe;* Charles Johnson drawing cartoons, and reading Hermann Hesse; Diane Johnson writing a novel at age ten, and reading Henry James; Philip Levine walking alone through his desolate neighborhood, and reading Dostoevsky; David Levering Lewis slipping through his father's book-lined study, and reading Lytton Strachey; Barry Lopez growing up in southern California, and reading Gerard Manley Hopkins; David McCullough tracing his family ancestry back to the Revolutionary War, and reading Willa Cather; Alice McDermott keeping a daily diary, and reading Emily Brontë; Cynthia Ozick dictating lyric poems to her mother, and then reading E. M. Forster; Grace Paley listening to classical music records, and reading Isaac Babel; Linda Pastan growing up an only child, and reading Tennyson; Katherine Paterson raised by missionary parents in China, and reading Alan Paton; and Robert Stone glued to science fiction drama on the radio, and reading Joseph Conrad.

Having lived with and through these interviews over the years, having heard Diane Osen's excitement and elation when she called me to check in after each new conversation, I am suppressing the temptation to reveal any more about them. To do so would be to deny a multitude of literary delights to you, the reader poised on the brink.

I will leave you with this confident guarantee: There are enough recommendations of influence in these pages to send you running to the bookstore or the public library, or—most delectably of all—

back to a leisurely ramble through your own bookshelves at home, in search of old favorites deserving a new look.

Autumn 2002
New York City

—

NEIL BALDWIN is the executive director of the National Book Foundation, sponsor of the National Book Awards. He is the author of several biographies, including, most recently, *Henry Ford and the Jews.*

THE BOOK
THAT CHANGED
MY LIFE

JAMES CARROLL

James Carroll, Winner of the 1996 National Book Award for his memoir An American Requiem: God, My Father, and the War That Came Between Us, *was born in Chicago in 1943 and grew up outside Washington, D.C., where his father worked as an FBI agent. After joining the military, his father became a lieutenant general in the air force and director of the Defense Intelligence Agency. Carroll attended Georgetown University before entering St. Paul's College, the Paulist Fathers' seminary in Washington, D.C. After his ordination to the priesthood in 1969, he served as the Catholic Chaplain at Boston University*

for five years before leaving the priesthood and pursuing a career as a writer. In the years since, he has published nine novels, including Mortal Friends, Prince of Peace, and The City Below, and written a weekly op-ed column for The Boston Globe. *In his most recent book, the critically acclaimed* Constantine's Sword: The Church and the Jews, *he chronicles the two-thousand-year-old battle of the Church against Judaism, while confronting the crisis of faith this tragedy has provoked in his own life.*

A Fellow of the American Academy of Arts and Sciences and a member of its Committee for International Security Studies, Carroll is a former chair and current member of the council of PEN/New England, as well as a Trustee of the Boston Public Library and a member of the Advisory Board of the International Center for Ethics, Justice, and Public Life at Brandeis University. He has held fellowships at the Kennedy School of Government at Harvard University and at Harvard Divinity School. He remains an Associate of Harvard's Belfer Center for Science and International Affairs, where he is at work on a history of the Pentagon. His tenth novel will be published in 2003. He lives in Boston with his wife, the novelist Alexandra Marshall, and their two grown children.

Hailed by the judges of the 1996 National Book Awards as a "flawlessly executed" memoir, An American Requiem, *tells the story of James Carroll's transformation from a passive, politically conservative seminarian into an outspoken critic of the war in Vietnam and proponent of civil rights—a transformation that divides him from his father even as it brings him closer to God. An unforgettable account of a son's struggle to claim his own political and religious identity,* An American Requiem *reveals that, in the author's words, the "very act of storytelling, of arranging memory and invention according to the structure of narrative, is by definition holy. . . . Telling our stories is what saves us; the story is enough."*

DIANE OSEN: You write in *An American Requiem* that as a young seminarian you started composing poems and stories to help salve your soul. Why do you suppose you turned to writing, instead of something else, to find that relief and release?

JAMES CARROLL: It was the accident, I suppose, of being in a setting in which reading and writing were at the heart of what I was doing, as opposed, for example, to being in the world of business, or the military, or some other career. I wasn't raised to be a book person, and to find myself in a world where I was expected to read seriously and write seriously in an academic setting, well, it was a first-time experience for me. Before entering the seminary, I had not encountered the life-changing potential of reading as a source of meaning, as a way of ordering one's inner life, and being rooted in the world.

DO: What are some of the books that had, for you, that kind of life-changing potential?

JC: I was very moved by *The Confessions of Saint Augustine*, which I was required to read. To my surprise, I identified with this great figure, as I recognized the details of his ordinary life in my own. The great self-accusation that Augustine brings to bear isn't of a crime; it isn't even what people often think it is, the sin of sexual license as a young man. It is the relatively mundane offense of taking an apple from somebody's orchard. This challenge to his conscience is the beginning of a journey from that mundane experience to a very profound intuition about the place of human beings in the world.

To read Plato and Aristotle, to track the ways in which they affected the thinkers of the West—largely Christian thinkers—was a really life-changing experience for me. I was changed again by reading the Existentialists, and Albert Camus was especially important to me. The tragic quality of his life was irresistible to a young man like me, but there were patterns even in his experience that I had learned how to look for.

For example, *The Confessions* is structured in such a way that the climax comes when Augustine's mother dies, and he is numb, paralyzed, frozen. He's unable to weep for her, and he recognizes his own great flaw: his inability to accept his mother's love. He looks back on his whole life and sees that it's been one long flight from her. That epiphany breaks open the emotional paralysis, and he finally weeps for her. And in allowing his love for his mother to overwhelm him, and at last to feel her love, he recognizes that all along this has been God's love. Augustine goes on to take that experience of human love and develop the first great theology of the Trinity. The gospel of John had said that God is love, but Augustine describes exactly what that could mean.

I went from *The Confessions* to Camus's novel *L'Etranger*, where the main character is accused of murder, but what he understands to be his real crime is that his mother has just died and he was unable to weep at her funeral. Whether Camus was consciously using this image he shares with a fellow North African from 1,700 years before or not, my discovery of this common, simple intuition about the importance of love—well, for a young man who was full of feelings but not sure what to make of them, it was a liberation. To feel licensed to have these powerful feelings of openness to life, and to be told, first by Augustine, that it's sacred, and then, by Camus, that it goes to the heart of secular human life, was a tremendous liberation—especially since I'd grown up in a Puritan culture where the basic message is that such feelings are not to be trusted.

It seems odd, but to be in a room, alone, with the door closed, reading books, encountering books, and then to understand that you can leave the room and be the person that you've been wanting to be all along—it was a great thing. And to go from something like that into a theological exploration of who God is—it was an unbelievably exhilarating time, and every book you read in such a context would send you into two more books.

DO: You've been writing novels for many years now. What inspired you at this point in your life to write a memoir?

JC: Two things: the aging and deaths of my parents, and the coming to maturity of my children. It seemed very important to me that my children should come into adulthood with a fuller sense of who their grandparents were, and in particular, of what my father's struggle was. My children knew my father as a senile old man. That was such a source of grief to me—to see my son Patrick's eyes cloud with fear at my father's arrival.

I later understood that there were larger movements, as well. It's no coincidence that while I was at work on that book, the United States of America was at the final stage of lifting the embargo on Vietnam. It took us twenty years to accomplish that, and my work was simply one person's version of that broad, national movement. Ending the war, and my own experience of it, was also part of the motive. What I was trying to do was write this very particular story of the people of my generation, who came of age with, first, the paranoia about communism, the assumptions of the Cold War, and the dread of nuclear conflict; and then, the civil rights movement, the coming of John F. Kennedy, the coming of Martin Luther King, and the end of it all, both in the assassinations and in the war.

DO: I imagine that the act of writing *An American Requiem* brought you to a lot of other new insights, as well. What was your most surprising discovery?

JC: I was surprised by, and quite relieved by, the order in my life. To discover, for example, that my father's public life begins in the act of tracking down a draft dodger who was a notorious criminal in the thirties in Chicago, and to go from that to the end of my father's public life, when he sticks his neck out for his draft dodger son, and recognized a classic reversal in that. Such reversal is the structure of narrative. The beautiful order of it, the way it says everything, really, about the distance my father had come in this life—to discover that order was very important to me, and very moving.

And that's just one of many, many epiphanies that I came upon in reflecting seriously on this family life story. To see the pattern—tragic, but nevertheless beautiful—that the Catholic peace movement should have played an important part in laying bare, and opposing, the crime of the Vietnam War: That was a perfect counterpoint to the way in which Cardinal Spellman and the Catholics in Saigon had laid the groundwork for the war. These patterns, by and large patterns of reversal, are built in, Aristotle says, to the human narrative impulse. To discover these patterns in my own and my family story was to draw meaning out of meaninglessness, and it was quite exhilarating.

DO: I want to ask you about a couple of passages toward the end of *American Requiem*. You write, "Telling our stories is what saves us. The story is enough." And later, "The very act of storytelling, of arranging memory and invention according to the structure of narrative is, by definition, holy." Can you talk a little bit more about your sense of storytelling as a holy act?

JC: It's what I was saying to you before about discovering the order in what appeared to be, while going through it, a disordered and meaningless set of experiences. As a religious person, I see that order as a symbol of the order that the Creator of the Universe has planted in our lives. It's the essence of my faith. And it's why I'm very at home in the Biblical tradition that talks about the Word of God as the central manifestation of the way in which God is in the world. In that way the word "holy" is appropriate for me: This is what I take to be the essence of biblical faith. It's what it means to be a part of what we call "the people of the book."

   In other words, my notion of narrative informs my faith, and my notion of faith informs my idea of what writing is for.

DO: Having said that, what do you think of Allen Tate's observation, which you recount in your memoir, that one can have the vocation of a priest or the vocation of a writer, but not both?

JC: There are some people who've made a good life of the priesthood while being seriously committed writers. Daniel Berrigan is the most important example that comes to mind, and, obviously, Gerard Manley Hopkins.

   But it's no accident that Daniel Berrigan has to live in the Church as a kind of rebel. George Orwell said once, facetiously and displaying his bias, that "few Catholics have been any good as novel writers, and those that were, were bad Catholics." It's a bit of a joke, of course. But there's some kind of truth to it. I left the priesthood because I didn't want to spend the rest of my life in rebellion against my boss. A writer's final authority has, finally, to be his or her own conscience and imagination. You can't worry about what other people are going to make of what you write. And you can't be trying to get permission from somebody.

DO: In reading two other works that have changed your life—Tim O'Brien's *The Things They Carried* and James Joyce's "The Dead"— I was struck by the presence of ghosts, who play an important role in your book, as well. O'Brien's narrator says, "We kept the dead alive with stories." Is that, for you, another function of narrative?

JC: I'd say Tim O'Brien puts it quite beautifully. It's not at all an accident to me that the followers of Jesus, who were in grief when He died and went away, were able to claim a new life, to feel united as a community, when they gathered to tell the story about what they had experienced of Him. It's the story that brings Jesus back. This is a religion that is built on the impulse to tell a story.

What I love about O'Brien is the way in which he's constantly pushing against the boundaries, in a way that I don't, between the science of fact and the truth of the imagination. There's an almost sinister quality to it, but nevertheless a playfulness to the author's work in *The Things They Carried*, where he's teasing the reader constantly. Is this real? No. Is *this* real? This is real. And at the end we say, Well, did it really happen?

And by then, of course, if O'Brien has succeeded, we're not asking that anymore. We're asking another question: What is the meaning of this story that we've just experienced? A person of faith comes to the end of a reading of the New Testament in a similar way. When you're really ready to believe in the Good News you stop asking, Was that tomb really empty? You get beyond that question, to the question of, What is the Resurrection in my life?

Even when the story is painful, the telling of it opens us to a level of experience, a transcendent level—which is why, for me, James Joyce's "The Dead" is so powerful. The trivial and banal socializing of the Dublin middle class is transformed into something else when Gretta tells her husband, Gabriel, the story of her first love. And even though, at one level, that's a terrible thing for Gabriel to hear—he realizes Gretta loves the memory of this man in a way that she will never love him—that story opens Gabriel to a new realm, where he understands something about the mystery of human experience.

That is the meaning of those magnificent last three pages of the story, where Gabriel stands by the window and is aware of the snow falling all across Ireland, and understands that the snow is blanketing the earth and time. There's a kind of acceptance, a profoundly beautiful acceptance of human experience, which is his response to his wife's story. Even if we never see snow falling, or sense it falling the way it falls at the end of "The Dead," still, who can finish that story without being somehow made more aware of the poignancy of mortality, the poignancy of the passage of time, the fact that we're all somehow in the position of that man, loving what we love, or who we love, more than we can ever be loved in return? And it is all available to us by the telling of the story.

DO: *An American Requiem* opens with your sermon about bones burned by napalm, and ends with the bones of your father being laid to rest—making it impossible, I think, for readers not to ask, Why are we here? What else do you hope your readers will take away from this book?

JC: The single most important ambition I have for this book is that a reader will be inspired to do a version of the same thing for his or her own life—to discover the order of it. To understand that conflict, which we think of as a terrible thing, is actually at the heart of the structures of our lives. To understand that reversals, which we think of as bad things, in fact give us the structure of meaning, when we go back and look at them.

There is sadness in life, but—and this is the mystery of the tragic form—when we tell the story, even informally, to another person, the beauty of it can become what we take away, what we are moved by, and why we love it. What transforms the merely sad into something tragic—and therefore beautiful, and therefore saving, and therefore, in some odd way, joyful—is the telling of the story. It's what makes us human beings. Everybody was put here to do this.

BOOKS BY JAMES CARROLL
> *Madonna Red*
> *Mortal Friends*
> *Fault Lines*
> *Family Trade*
> *Prince of Peace*
> *Supply of Heroes*
> *Firebird*
> *Memorial Bridge*
> *The City Below*
> *An American Requiem*
> *Constantine's Sword: The Church and the Jews, A History*

Readers who want to learn more about James Carroll are encouraged to seek out some of the books that have shaped his writing life:
> "The Dead," James Joyce
> *The Things They Carried,* Tim O'Brien
> *The Confessions of St. Augustine*
> *The Stranger* (*L'Etranger*), Albert Camus
> *The Four Quartets,* T. S. Eliot

DON DELILLO

Don DeLillo, *a three-time Finalist for the National Book Award and winner for his 1985 novel* White Noise, *was born in 1936 and grew up in the Bronx. After graduating from Fordham College he worked as an advertising copywriter for several years before becoming a freelance writer. Several years later he started working on his first novel,* Americana, *about a television executive who leaves his unsatisfying job and marriage to find an authentic identity.*

The first American recipient of the prestigious Jerusalem Prize, and the winner of the Irish Times International Fiction Prize and a PEN/Faulkner Award, Mr. DeLillo has continued to explore the ways in which mass culture and technology obstruct the search for meaning in the atomic age. Nowhere is that search more hauntingly evoked than in his epic novel Underworld, *a Finalist for the National Book Award in 1997. Dizzying in its scope and dazzling in its effects, the novel interweaves the secret history of the Cold War and its "devil twin," nuclear waste, with the secret trajectory of Bobby Thomson's legendary home-run ball in the 1951 Dodgers-Giants pennant race. At the center of the novel is Nick Shay, erstwhile Dodgers fan, present owner of the mythic baseball, and Bronx native, who can neither escape nor understand his past. His efforts to remake his identity in a world that has replaced God with "radioactivity, the power of alpha particles and the all-knowing systems that shape them" is at the heart of this unforgettable novel about the mystery of loss and the transcendence of faith.*

DIANE OSEN: How is it that you became a writer?

DON DELILLO: It's a bit of a mystery, because I didn't write at all as a child, and I did not do much reading, either. I liked to play. The minute I got out of school I started playing street games, card games, alley games, rooftop games, fire escape games, punch ball, stickball, handball, stoop ball, and a hundred other games. I read comic books and I listened to the radio. No one read to anyone else at home. That's why we had the radio; the radio read to us all.

In high school, I'd occasionally pick up a book that was not part of a school assignment. I remember reading *I Escaped from Devil's Island.* I remember reading Bram Stoker's *Dracula.* And my memories of these books have a physical quality. I can still see the broken type in the small brown hardcover copy of *Dracula,* and I can still see the sun-browned pages of the paperback version of *Devil's Island.*

Eventually, I began to read a number of contemporary American writers. I read James T. Farrell—*The Studs Lonigan Trilogy.* I read most of Hemingway and Faulkner. I read the short stories of Flannery O'Connor in the collection *A Good Man Is Hard to Find.* A little later I read *The Complete Poems of Hart Crane* in a paperback edition I still have—ninety-five cents. I suppose this period of my life as a reader culminated with James Joyce's *Ulysses.*

I wrote some short stories in my late teens and through most of my twenties—haphazardly. I did not have a strong sense of writerly ambition. I was about two years into my first novel, *Americana,* when it occurred to me that I could conceivably be a writer.

DO: What inspired you to undertake a novel at all?

DD: It was largely an impulse growing out of a specific moment. I was in Southwest Harbor on Mount Desert Island in Maine, look-ing down a street filled with elms and maples and old homes. And there was something in the moment. Some mystery that made me feel I had to write about it. And even though it took me, oh, I don't know, two months before I even put a word on paper, even the title of the novel was implicit in that moment.

DO: Was there a specific moment that inspired *Underworld,* as well?

DD: This novel is the only one that had such a specific starting point. And the starting point was the front page of *The New York Times* for October 4, 1951. I looked at the page on a microfilm reader roughly forty years after the occurrence of the two head-lined events on the front page. The first headline was about the ball game described in the novel's prologue—a famous play-off game featuring the New York Giants and the Brooklyn Dodgers. And the second headline concerned the testing of an atomic bomb by the Soviet Union. These two juxtaposed headlines struck me with the force of a revelation. I felt there was something here I wanted to understand and write about.

DO: The game of course becomes something of an obsession for several characters in *Underworld,* especially for Nick, whose trans-formation from a tough Bronx street kid into a Latin-speaking waste management executive is, for me, one of the marvels of the novel. How did you go about finding his voice? And why did you decide, for the first time in any of your novels, to write about the Bronx of your adolescence?

DD: I wrote about those streets and those people in my earlier short stories, but I don't think I was nearly adept enough to do justice to the subject. So after thirty-five years or so, I've gone back and thought hard and remembered deeply. I knew the landscape intimately and found considerable pleasure in drawing on distant memories of that period. I found I could reclaim the smallest moment, even the most glancing encounter. I could hear the voices, recall the curious slang words, the southern Italian dialect words, the speech rhythms and idiosyncrasies.

It occurred to me, as I was reading the galleys of the Bronx chapters in Part Six, that there were not nearly so many compound words, invented words, hyphenated words, words fused together, as there were in the rest of the manuscript. There is a kind of ease and directness of address, which flows from the experience in those streets. It's not stark, but there's a difference between the writing in Part Six and the writing in the rest of the book. And curiously, this reflects the journey that Nick Shay takes from adolescence to adulthood, from dark, narrow, working-class streets to a sundazzled landscape outside Phoenix.

DO: The power of words to create and re-create the world is exceptionally potent in this novel. Nick, for example, learns new words because he believes it's the only way to escape the things that made him, and along similar lines, Louis says that wars can't be fought without acronyms.

DD: Well, you're certainly right that the power of language is a theme in this book. In Nick's case, you may have noticed that as an adult he has a slightly self-conscious approach to these matters. He will stare at the books on his bookshelf as a way of reassuring himself that he has, in fact, made a journey. And he will instruct his children in the definitions of words that are slightly remote. And, of course, the reader with luck makes a direct connection between those passages and the passage in which Nick and the Jesuit priest discuss the names of the parts of a shoe. A discussion, in a sense, that is theological, and that has a shaping effect on Nick. It occurs to him, as the perpetrator of a violent act, that what he needs to transcend this act, to uninvent and then remake himself, is a grip on language. And he not only self-consciously attempts to improve himself, but he even studies Latin as a token of depth and aspiring maturity.

A part of the book that I find telling is when he reflects on some of these matters and ultimately expresses his regret and longing for the days when he felt physically connected to the earth. The days when he had freedom to commit transgressive acts. And it's not a nostalgia for innocence, it's a nostalgia for guilt.

DO: What's interesting to me is Nick's belief that his father's disappearance is a failure from which no one in his family can escape.

DD: The book in some sense is about the mystery of loss—not just loss but the mystery of its durability, its character-defining depth, and the ways in which we embellish on it, adorn it, redecorate it. And, of course, there's a theme of bad luck.

DO: It seems to me that Marvin's obsessive pursuit of the ball is also about bad luck and the mystery of loss.

DD: Marvin Lundy is a morose sort of comedian. He has a pessimistic slant on life. Even when there is no bad luck in evidence, he foresees it. He is an obsessive collector of baseball memorabilia and he finally realizes that he is collecting these objects, that he is amassing these possessions against the prospect of future loss—deep emotional loss.

DO: One of the powerful forces acting on everyone in the novel is the underworld of technology. How do you think it affects our daily lives?

DD: I think that the massive, overarching, interconnected systems of technology tend to make us a little insecure, somewhat pliable, and susceptible to half-beliefs. I think technology drains us of convictions. It is so powerful and so sophisticated that we tend to lose some of our self-confidence in an almost imperceptible way.

DO: With so many underworlds already intersecting in the novel, what compelled you to invent the Eisenstein film called *Unterwelt* that Klara sees at Radio City?

DD: I suppose this is the artistic underworld, and almost the literal center of the novel. And I felt I needed a stronger Russian presence in the book. Since I wasn't writing the kind of Cold War novel that depends on spies and codes and so forth, I decided to do it this way, with a document.

The novel is actually filled with documents of various kinds. Songs, radio programs, TV programs, movies, paintings, photographs, disk jockey patter, the Lenny Bruce routines, which I did very purposefully as a way of adding a certain depth of texture, since this is how we receive most of our information to begin with.

The Eisenstein film functions on a number of levels. In one way, it's a semi-comical reference to the effects of radiation as they are seen in a Japanese science fiction movie. On a deeper level, it is a representation of the political repression of artists in the Soviet Union, which of course is something that Eisenstein experienced. On an even more personal and intimate level, it represents a kind of sexual self-repression that connects Eisenstein with J. Edgar Hoover. One can also work back from the Eisenstein film to the Bruegel painting [that transfixes Hoover at the ball game] in terms of grotesque suffering. And one can work forward from it to the damaged children of Kazakhstan in the epilogue.

DO: Speaking of Kazakhstan, in the epilogue Viktor tells Nick that waste is the devil twin of the bomb, because it embodies the under-history of the nuclear arms race. I assume that's a view you share—how did it develop?

DD: I'd been thinking about garbage for twenty years, and stopped thinking about it; I decided I didn't know what this was all leading to. Then the subject reasserted itself. I'm not sure why.

In the prologue there are a number of passages in which fans at the ballpark throw litter from the stands. It occurred to me at some point that this was the bland version of garbage, just pieces of paper. But as it turns out, this is the beginning of a kind of evolving theme in the book. And as the novel progresses, the garbage becomes more and more offensive and more dangerous. This is why in the Sputnik passages we see a number of references to ordinary household products and the dangers they bear. So that this danger in technology—a kind of innate danger—is visible even in the most innocuous objects. The danger finally culminates in nuclear waste being destroyed by a nuclear weapon.

DO: You mentioned Lenny Bruce earlier. Are his routines in the book also invented? And why did you include them?

DD: There are about two and a half sentences that are Lenny Bruce's; the rest is invented. I'm not sure how Lenny Bruce entered the book. I do know that I felt I needed to do a piece of comedy about the Cold War. And Lenny Bruce, to my way of thinking, was a somewhat unacknowledged force in that culture.

DO: I keep hearing him shout at the audience, "We're all gonna die!" Do you think Americans are still as terrified of the bomb as he was? Or have we gotten so lost in other forms of technology that we don't think about it anymore?

DD: We don't think about the immediate danger of the bomb. In fact, the time is coming when we will begin to feel nostalgia for the Cold War. For its certainties and its biblical sense of awesome confrontation. A character in the novel says that someday tourists will make journeys to Plutonium National Park. In fact, I believe this will happen, in one form or another. It is probably already happening.

In those years we lived through two levels of danger. The possibility of a nuclear exchange between the United States and the Soviet Union. And the psychological sense of randomness and ambiguity that flowed from the assassinations and social disruptions of the 1960s. This latter state of mind is still an aspect of the culture and it's precisely this unease that will bring about a wistfulness for the days of clearly defined confrontation.

DO: One final question: On the subject of atomic war, Klara says to an interviewer early in the novel that "if you maintain a force in the world that comes into people's sleep, you are exercising a meaningful power." Having dreamed about *Underworld* several times now, I wonder whether as a novelist you aspire to that kind of power.

DD: A novelist would certainly be delighted to hear that his book has such a power, but it is not something he consciously aspires to. Speaking for myself, I was trying to survive day by day, and had absolutely no sense of what impact this book, or any other book I've written, would make in the world. People have suggested to me that this is the culmination of my work. I honestly don't know. I don't want to know. I'll just do what comes next.

BOOKS BY DON DELILLO

Americana
End Zone
Great Jones Street
Ratner's Star
Players
Running Dog
The Names
White Noise
Libra
The Day Room (play)
Mao II
Underworld
Valparaiso (play)
The Body Artist

Readers who wish to learn more about Don DeLillo may want to explore some of the books that have shaped his life as a writer:

Ulysses, James Joyce
A Good Man Is Hard to Find, Flannery O'Connor
The Complete Poems of Hart Crane
The Studs Lonigan Trilogy, James T. Farrell
The works of Ernest Hemingway and William Faulkner

E. L. DOCTOROW

Like the narrator of his National Book Award–winning novel World's Fair, *novelist, essayist, and dramatist E(dgar) L(aurence) Doctorow was born and raised in New York City during the Depression. After graduating with honors from Kenyon College in 1952, he did postgraduate work at Columbia University, served in the U.S. Army and returned to New York City where he took a job as a reader for a motion picture company. He went on to become an editor with The New American Library and subsequently editor-in-chief of The Dial Press before leaving publishing to pursue writing full-time.*

His first novel, Welcome to Hard Times, *published in 1960, was both a parody of the Western genre, as well as a compelling exploration of the moral fate of its characters. His interest in the American experience—and in unconventional narratives and moral values— also distinguishes the novels that have followed, including* The Book of Daniel, Loon Lake, *and* Billy Bathgate—*all Finalists for The National Book Award—as well as* Ragtime *and* The Waterworks. *His most recent novel,* City of God, *was published to wide acclaim in 2000.*

Published in 1985, World's Fair *reflects vividly Mr. Doctorow's belief that "art and life make each other." Characterized by the author as an "illusion of a memoir," the novel traces in uncanny detail the daily experiences of a Jewish boy from the Bronx named Edgar, who occasionally shares the narration with his mother, Rose, brother, Donald, and aunt, Frances. The story of Edgar's growth from a toddler to a nine-year-old, with more than a passing acquaintance with sex and death, is "E. L. Doctorow's portrait of the artist as a young child," observes critic Richard Eder. "The author's alter ego, Edgar Altshuler, grows into an awareness that the world stretches far beyond the protective confines of a Bronx Jewish household. . . . Doctorow evokes Edgar's gradual maturing with something close to magic."*

In addition to the National Book Award, E. L. Doctorow is also the recipient of honors including the National Book Critics Circle Award (twice), the PEN/Faulkner Award, the John Guggenheim Fellowship, the Edith Wharton Citation for Fiction, and the William Dean Howells Medal of the American Academy and National Institute of Arts and Letters. In 1998, he was awarded the National Humanities Medal at the White House.

DIANE OSEN: The narrator of your novel *World's Fair* reads all the time—which makes him, by his own lights, a typical American boy. Were you a typical American boy, as well? And did you share Edgar's early interest in sea stories and adventure stories and stories about sports?

E. L. DOCTOROW: Yes. I was fortunate to grow up before television was all over America and in every home, and I was also fortunate to be part of a family of readers. This was during the Depression, when nobody had any money, but somehow there were books in the house, shelves and shelves of them. Books that were there before I was. My father would bring home new books, my mother borrowed books from the rental library, I was read to as a child, and as soon as I could read myself I was given a card for the public library. I read indiscriminately. I read Alexandre Dumas's swashbucklers, I read Dickens's *David Copperfield, A Tale of Two Cities,* Maupassant's stories, Jules Verne, Jack London, the Sherlock Holmes adventures, the Baseball Joe books—everything. And I would read in binges.

My grandfather, my father's father, was of the immigrant generation that came over in the 1880s. He was a great reader, a printer by trade and something of an intellectual, and he, too, had a considerable library. Not only books in English but Russian books and books in Yiddish. It was in his house that I first heard the name Tolstoy. Lev Tolstoy, my grandfather called him.

At any rate I remember one Sunday's visit with my parents to my grandfather's house. At this time I was very keen on horror stories, they were all I wanted to read. My father showed me one of my grandfather's books. He said to me, "You like all that horror stuff. Here's one called *The Green Hand.* That sounds horrible enough. You want to try it?" I said I did, and so while all the grown-ups were having tea and talking, I sat in the corner and opened this book. Of course, it wasn't a horror story about a green hand, it was a novel about a novice aboard a sailing ship, a greenhand. So as a result of that sly trick of my father's, I was off on stories about the sea. That particular volume was one of a set of sea novels my grandfather had. I was to go through them all. And that's the way it went, from one passion to another. Mark Twain, of course, Frank Baum's *Wizard of Oz* books. I stumbled on *Candide* one day, a somewhat menacing book to a child. I remember reading an illustrated version of *Don Quixote* and another time taking home a library book that I thought had an intriguing title: *The Idiot.* So I read it.

Of course, somewhere in all of this I began to identify with the authors who were writing these books. That is to say, there was something in my mind that could appreciate the art of those narratives that I found so riveting. I don't know if that occurs to all young people as they read, but certainly for writers-to-be, there's that additional line of inquiry in the brain that goes along with the reading: How is this done? Could I do this? A little green shoot of literary ambition, barely acknowledged, almost unconscious, in fact.

DO: After you graduated from Kenyon College, you studied drama and acting at Columbia University before you became a script reader at Columbia Pictures. How did those experiences shape your approach to storytelling?

ELD: When I went to Kenyon we were very much under the influence of the New Criticism. The poet and critic John Crowe Ransom taught there. We did textual criticism at Kenyon the way they played football at Ohio State. In the long run it was valuable training, but it called upon resources of the mind, analytical capacities, that are not what you want at the forefront of your mind when you write.

I was a student actor as well, at Kenyon and at Columbia University, and I became, for a while, seriously interested in writing for the theater. But the novelist doesn't rely on other people to realize his work, as the playwright does. And so I turned to fiction writing. By the time I got that reader's job at Columbia Pictures I was well along in a novel, a more-or-less autobiographical novel. But it took me some time to work up the courage to admit it was not working. It was not working at all. Because I was a professional reader, I knew how many bad books were being published and so I was not about to be discouraged. I had learned also, working under deadlines, how to synopsize a novel by reconstructing its story with economy, as a tale told on two single-spaced pages, which really sharpened my editorial skills. But here's the thing that happened that was really crucial: In that job, you see, I had to read a lot of westerns. The film companies were making them, they were a reliable movie product. And so whatever was being published in the genre had to be covered. All this vomitous stuff.

One day I sat down and wrote a western story, because I thought I could lie about the West better than the people I was reading. It was a parody, a western to end all westerns. And then the man I was working for, the story editor, read it and said, This is good; you ought to turn it into a novel. Of course, "parody" as a term covers a wide range of possibilities, and somewhere along the line I saw the book developing not as a satire but as something done in counterpoint. What intrigued me finally was the idea of taking a disreputable genre and making something out of it, writing quite seriously against the reader's expectations.

This book taught me something about myself: I was not the kind of writer who could walk into a party and listen to the talk and see how the people were dressed and what they were up to and who was sleeping with whom and then go home and write a story about it. I was not given to literary realism; I was not a reporter, I needed distance, I needed a dramatized voice to work in. Whatever light came to me would have to shine through a prism of invention. Even in *World's Fair*, the most autobiographical of the books, I used myself as material for the composition, as I would use anything else from any other source.

DO: What led you to write "A Writer in the Family"? And how did that story, which features some of the same characters and situations, evolve into *World's Fair*?

ELD: I actually did lose my father, like the boy in that story, but I wasn't that young; I was twenty-four when my father died. And I was asked by my aunts to write a letter pretending to be my father, so that my old grandmother, his mother, who was in a nursing home, would be spared the news of his death. The idea, you see, would have been that my father and all of us had moved far away, out of state. And I knew that was wrong, so I refused. They were able to withhold the news of his death easily enough on their own, if that's what they wanted to do.

I thought about that incident for many years and realized that because I had refused my aunts' request there was no story. But if a fictional kid said yes, he'd do it, you had a story. That's an example of how you transform material from your own life. As I wrote the piece the age was lowered to thirteen, and as the writer in the family—that is, as a boy who'd shown up very well in his various school compositions—this boy was able to imagine his father living out West in Arizona and writing what life was like for the family out there in the 1950s. And all the time they're still in the Bronx and mourning the father and visiting his grave.

Well, you see, one thing leads to another, and it seemed perfectly logical next time out to be writing about that same family while the father was still alive and healthy. That would bring the family back to the thirties and forties. And with a few age adjustments, getting into the family dynamics there in the Depression, and having the young writer in the family winning a prize in the World's Fair essay contest on the theme of the Typical American Boy that allows them all to go to the Fair.

DO: You've written about the novel as a "false document," Kenneth Rexroth's phrase for a work of fiction, like Defoe's *Robinson Crusoe,* that gains authority by representing itself as a factual account. What inspired you to write *World's Fair* as a novel disguised as a memoir, interspersed with accounts by family members?

ELD: Novelists have always tried to give their work authority by means of whatever strategy seems appropriate to their times. So Defoe's strategy with *Robinson Crusoe* was to deny his own authorship. There was a well-known castaway living in London in those days by the name of Alexander Selkirk; it was simple enough for Defoe to invent another castaway whose actual living existence was proposed as if Defoe had only edited his book. Cervantes did the same sort of thing with *Don Quixote* when he claimed—in Book Nine, I think—to have bought the manuscript for six reals in a shop in Toledo and to have had it translated from the Aramaic.

One of the devices used in *World's Fair* to persuade the reader of its authority is the taped interview, the interposition of passages in which members of the family speak in their own voices, as apparently transcribed. This was my acknowledgment of the power I had recognized, around that time, in the collections of oral histories that were being published—how impressive I found the testimonies of supposedly ordinary people reporting on their lives.

DO: In your essay "False Documents," you also mention the critic Walter Benjamin, who could have been discussing *World's Fair* when he wrote, in one of his essays, that "language shows clearly that memory is not an instrument for exploring the past but its theater." What can you tell us in this regard about the extraordinary voice of the novel, and its relationship to the major themes of the book?

ELD: I would certainly accept the notion of memory as a dramatization of the past, which is what Benjamin is talking about. But I'm not sure I can answer your question. I will say the language you use is a decision you make in the depths of your brain before you even begin. A voice comes to you as something complete, with its own diction and its own level of syntactical simplicity or complexity. And it's your engine. Certainly, you might have an idea for something, but if you don't find the voice it won't go.

World's Fair begins as an adult's voice looking back on childhood circumstances; but as the child grows older and becomes articulate, the voice of the narration actually becomes younger, even though it's still, presumably and conventionally, the voice of an adult recalling his childhood.

It's hard, though, to really analyze the connection between the language and the themes of a novel. I mean, the people who do this work are perhaps the last people in the world who should be consulted about it. When I started, I knew a lot more about writing than I do now. Now I just do it. And I think that's probably the experience of people who have the calling, as they work at it year after year.

There are things you do that you don't understand as an intention. It was a critic who described *World's Fair* as a portrait of the artist as a young boy. I had never thought of it that way, but it's a fair way to look at it.

DO: In a recent interview, the historian David McCullough told me that he thinks of himself as "a writer who has found in the past an opportunity for self-expression that for many reasons, some of which I'm probably not able to understand myself, appeals to me more than any other." What is it about the past that has so often appealed to you as a writer?

ELD: Well, there again, it wasn't until *Ragtime*, which was my fourth novel, that I realized that I was tending to deal with material from the past. It was my editor who told me. And it's true that you can take my books and arrange them in a certain order and get one writer's vision of the past hundred-twenty or so years of American life. This was never planned; I never set out with an overriding scheme or ambition to do this. The one thing I realized was that for me, as an urban writer, a period of time could be as useful an organizing principle for a novel as a sense of place. I must have figured that out unconsciously. That in this huge and volatile society very little connects us—that perhaps all we have to bind us are a few historical images. Nevertheless I would deny that I write historical novels. All novels are set in the past, if you think about it. I'll define a novel as historical if it makes literary history.

DO: Both *World's Fair* and *Billy Bathgate* dramatize the ways in which, as Edgar might put it, a boy aspires to the power of himself, and learns the world. This is, of course, a theme that Mark Twain explores, as well, in *The Prince and the Pauper, Tom Sawyer,* and *Huckleberry Finn,* among other books. Why is this theme so resonant for you? And what else about *The Prince and the Pauper* in particular, and Mark Twain in general, has captured your imagination over the years?

ELD: Well, as for Mark Twain, all children begin with *Tom Sawyer.* Try to imagine the tremendous impact that a book like *Tom Sawyer* must have on a child. Twain knew that boys are averse to soap and water. That they like to torment insects and cats. That they like small things they can treasure, coins, odd pieces of metal, anything that glitters. He understood that children traditionally are repositories of the tawdriest myths in society, that they play around with the idea of ghosts and the use of incantations to drive away warts and so on.

Then, of course, a child recognizes the underlying justice of the book's outcome, since Tom is a seemingly bad boy who is really good—which is the way we all feel about ourselves as children; always we are misunderstood. Tom stands between the totally anarchic Huck Finn and the goody-good half brother Sid, who is really quite malevolent and deceitful as he obeys all the rules. So there is a moral hierarchy in the book any child recognizes. I think that among the major American authors, Twain is the most loved because of the way in this book and in *Huckleberry Finn* he founded a moral universe from the lives of children.

In fact, a good proportion of Twain's work is devoted to taking children quite seriously, no matter how much fun he might be having. And what you find in *The Prince and the Pauper* is perhaps the most symbolic presentation of the democratic spirit you can imagine, because the two boys, prince and pauper, are finally interchangeable: Tom Canty functions eventually quite well as the Prince, and the Prince in his turn adapts rather well to the life of poverty and rags. What is being said is terribly anti-European and anti-monarchical: Twain is proposing that a society of class distinctions is essentially a fraud. The Prince learns some of this and goes back to his life, where he will rule as an enlightened monarch because of his experience. Of course, one could say that nothing has really changed in the way that society is structured. But what a child can take from this book is a strengthened belief in himself or herself, no matter how humble his circumstances. Mark Twain was a great moralist, and enough of a genius to build his morality into his books, with humor and wit and—in the case of *The Prince and the Pauper*—wonderful plotting.

I'll tell you something that I think I learned from Mark Twain:

There are built-in advantages to writing from a child's point of view. You are allowed to express wonder and amazement for all the ordinary things in the world that most adults don't see or feel anymore. And you can find yourself steering a vehicle that almost drives itself, the bildungsroman. It's an unbeatable form of literary transportation.

DO: You've talked about the growing isolation of what you've called our "print culture" and also about the ways in which politicians and journalists and professional spinmeisters are increasingly appropriating the techniques of novelists for their own ends. What do novelists have to do in order to reclaim fiction as the right and proper source of truth?

ELD: Well, the image I came up with twenty years ago was that we were being put out on a reservation, with a remote little plot of land to cultivate. The idea was that the fiction writer should write to reclaim his territory—his territory being the world, of course, the universe. But you know, what propels a writer is what resists any kind of advice. And it should. Whatever any of us writes should suggest our helplessness to write anything but what we've written.

DO: What propelled you to write your newest novel, *City of God*?

ELD: Just that—its time had come. I was helpless to write anything else. The nonlinear approach of *The Book of Daniel* and *Loon Lake,* and to a certain extent, *Lives of the Poets,* is here, too. *City of God* is the workbook or daybook of a writer at the end of the millennium. Almost inevitably, he's a repository of the predominating ideas and themes and historical disasters of the century. *City of God* is the life of his mind. He lives in New York and learns that a large crucifix that's been stolen from an Episcopal church on the Lower East Side of New York City has reappeared on the roof of a progressive synagogue on the Upper West Side. Sensing that there's a possible novel in this mystery the writer cultivates the acquaintance of the church's priest and the synagogue's rabbi and follows them in their effort to figure out who has done this and what it means. That is the book's magnet—what everything else in the writer's mind lines up on.

DO: One final question. You've said that "a book can affect consciousness... [and] create constituencies that have their own effect on history." I'm wondering how you hope your books will affect history, and what kinds of constituencies you hope they'll inspire.

ELD: I was speaking as a critic, a reader.

I wouldn't want to speculate about my own work. It's foolish for a writer to think of such things. It's far wiser to feel that you've done the best you can, and that whatever happens is out of your hands.

BOOKS BY E. L. DOCTOROW

Welcome to Hard Times
Big as Life
The Book of Daniel
Ragtime
Drinks Before Dinner (play)
Loon Lake
Lives of the Poets: Six Stories and a Novella
World's Fair
Billy Bathgate
Jack London, Hemingway and the Constitution (selected essays)
The Waterworks
City of God

CHARLES JOHNSON

Charles Johnson, Winner of the 1990 National Book Award for Fiction for his novel Middle Passage, *was born and raised in Evanston, Illinois. After earning bachelor's and master's degrees from Southern Illinois University, he worked during the 1970s as a cartoonist and journalist while preparing his first novel,* Faith and the Good Thing. *Among his other works are the novels* Oxherding Tale *and* Dreamer; *the short-story collections* The Sorcerer's Apprentice *and* Soulcatcher and Other Stories; Being and Race: Black Writing Since 1970, *a work of aesthetics that won a 1989 Governor's Award for Literature; and two collections of comic art,* Black Humor *and* Half-Past Nation Time. *He is the co-editor of* Black Men Speaking; *the co-author of* Africans in America: America's Journey through Slavery, *the companion book for the influential PBS television series; and co-author of* King: The Photobiography of Martin Luther King, Jr.

A Ph.D. in philosophy and a 1998 MacArthur Fellow, Dr. Johnson teaches fiction at the University of Washington, where he holds an endowed chair, the S. Wilson and Grace M. Pollock Professorship for Excellence in English. He has received honorary doctoral degrees from Southern Illinois University, Northwestern University, and the State University of New York at Stony Brook. The recipient of honors, including a Lifetime Achievement Award from the Corporate Council for the Arts and the Northwest Writers Association's 2001 Achievement Award, he is also one of twelve influential black authors portrayed in a special series of stamps issued in Asia, South America, and Africa in 1997. A member of the Modern Library's Editorial Board and a judge for prizes, including the National Book Award and the Pulitzer Prize, he is the author of numerous scholarly articles and reviews, as well as twenty screenplays, including Booker, *which won the international Prix Jeunesse Award and a Writers Guild Award. He was named one of the best short-story writers in America in a late 1980s survey conducted by the University of Southern California.*

Middle Passage, *set on a rundown slave ship under the command of a deranged captain, charts the efforts of Rutherford Calhoun, a recently freed slave and stowaway, to discover and embrace an authentic identity. Incorporating elements of a slave narrative, picaresque tale, sea yarn, and bildungsroman, the novel is informed, says critic Arend Flick, by a "remarkably generous thesis: that racism generally, and the institution of slavery in particular, might best be seen as having arisen . . . from a deep fissure that characterizes Western thought in general: our tendency to split the world into competing categories." The novel's triumph, he avers, can be found in Rutherford's unforgettable passage beyond divisive dualities toward unity—and in the novelist's skillful blending of philosophy and art, which in* Middle Passage *become one.*

DIANE OSEN: I know you grew up sharing an unusually eclectic home library with your mom. What were some of the books that most impressed you as a child?

CHARLES JOHNSON: Among my mother's books, which came from three book clubs, was Richard Wright's *Black Boy,* which was not taught in my high school and probably not in most high schools. She also had a book on yoga, which I thought was really interesting. It's where I first encountered meditation, and it's in my library now. And there was a book about the American theater from 1900 to 1955, with stills from the productions; I used to stare at that quite a lot. Those were books in her library that I found intriguing.

I was in book clubs of my own. And I read a book a week, I remember, starting probably from my freshman year in high school. I would spend about an hour at a little newsstand that had lots of paperback books, selecting what might look interesting to me for that particular week. I remember one summer I read the *Studs Lonigan* trilogy by James T. Farrell. What was interesting to me as a thirteen-year-old was that he was talking about places I knew, because they were just across the border from Evanston in Chicago.

I read genre fiction: science fiction, all the James Bond novels, westerns and Plutarch's *Lives of the Noble Grecians;* it was very much whatever appealed to me every week. I was also attracted to adventure stories, going all the way back to Homer's *Odyssey.* I liked stories that were imaginative; I liked stories that made me think; I liked stories that featured protagonists who faced dangers of one kind or another. That's what you find in *Black Boy,* actually; the dangers, of course, were the dangers of Mississippi segregation.

DO: By the time you graduated from high school, you were already a published cartoonist—which strikes me, at least, as an unusual background for a writer of literary fiction.

CJ: My obsession, from elementary school on, was drawing, because that was my primary talent and the one that my teachers recognized very early. When I was about twelve or thirteen, I decided I was going to be a visual artist, and that was my main focus for years, even before I started publishing cartoons at seventeen. And then it was my profession for seven years after that, from 1965 to 1972.

As I said, I loved reading and grew up in a house where there was always something to read; and those stories fed my imagination as an artist. I've never been able to engage in a kind of creative apartheid where I put, say, drawing in a box over here, and philosophy in a box over there, and literature in a box over here. They are all parts of life, which is one life, right?

You'll find, I think, that writers often began with a different discipline. Many began as musicians, like the late and great Ralph Ellison, who was a very accomplished musician and went to college on a scholarship. And there are other writers who have a visual talent; I think John Updike wanted to be a cartoonist. It's not unusual at all. What is unusual is for somebody to make sure that they don't let one talent fade away when they pick up another one. Actually, one discipline can prepare you for another. Music can prepare one for writing prose that is very metrical and cadenced and musical; as a matter of fact, the terms that we use for prosody in English come from music. One creative area, I think, cross-fertilizes another.

DO: In what ways has your work as a visual artist cross-fertilized your work as a writer?

CJ: Well, you know, even to this day, I still insist on drawing. I do two cartoons a month for *Black Issues in Higher Education*. For me, it's a real, important need. I have to draw because it's a way of telling a story.

When I do a drawing, I have to first think intellectually about it—what the composition is going to look like and what the gag is going to be. Then I have to be the costume designer. I have to be the hairstylist. I have to be the prop person. And I have to do the directing. If I were working on a film, I'd be the whole crew.

The same thing is true of writing, because it almost requires thinking the same way. After he read [my novel] *Dreamer,* my friend Ishmael Reed said to me, "The descriptions were what really impressed me—is that because you're a cartoonist?" And I said, Well, I do think about things like the quality of light as it strikes the characters and creates shadows around them. I think about detail as minutely as I do when I'm drawing. When I'm writing, my whole process of revision is largely devoted to increasing the specificity of everything that is there, to try to see more vividly and with more detail in my imagination. I tell my students all the time, You've got to be generous in the details that you give in your writing—and the best way to be generous is to be specific.

I truly believe all the arts are interconnected. I think that there is creative philosophy as well. And I believe that literature and philosophy are sister disciplines and always have been.

DO: Is that belief one of the things that's led you to devote yourself to creating what you've called "a genuine philosophical black literature"?

CJ: When I started writing, I began with one specific purpose in mind, and that was to expand what was called black philosophical fiction, or even more importantly, American philosophical fiction. It is not a tradition in twentieth-century American literature that offers many examples.

I think there are three practitioners who gave us a foundation for a genuinely philosophical black American literature. One is Jean Toomer, whose wonderful book *Cane* started the Harlem Renaissance in 1923. The second person, of course, is Richard Wright, who was a genius, in my opinion. He's called the father of modern black literature and everybody talks about him in terms of racial fiction and protest fiction, but there is much more going on: Wright is concerned with ideas, and how those ideas impact on our daily lives; you couldn't have a better model. The third person is his colleague Ralph Ellison, whose *Invisible Man* is a wonderful exploration of perception and blindness.

I looked at black American literature and I said, There is something here that I can make a contribution to. Every novel that I've written, every story that I've written, I hope advances that wing of American literature in some way.

DO: Herman Melville, of course, is considered one of America's most important philosophical novelists of the nineteenth century, and Jack London clearly had in mind his books about the sea when he wrote *The Sea-Wolf.* How did these narratives come to play such an important role in your novel about an actual and metaphysical sea journey, *Middle Passage?*

CJ: As I've said, I've always been drawn to those stories that maximize suspense and adventure. And I found Melville to be engaging on an intellectual level. In "Benito Cereno," he is exploring one of the great issues of the nineteenth century: slavery and the slave trade. Whether or not he's coming to conclusions that would be satisfactory to late twentieth-century readers is another matter; I think of Melville more as an artist than as a social commentator.

In *The Sea-Wolf* you've also got things, the philosophies of Nietzsche and Marx, that make Wolf Larsen very interesting. He is a domineering figure on a ship that is a world in and of itself, and onto this ship comes an idealist innocent. Their intellectual dialogue engaged me very much.

But to talk about *Middle Passage,* I have to talk first about the novel that preceded it, *Oxherding Tale.* And to talk about that book, I have to back up to when I was an undergraduate.

At the school I was going to, Southern Illinois University, there were no Black Studies programs until around 1969, and no core of teachers prepared to teach those classes, so the graduate students taught them. One day, one of the graduate students—this was in a history class—put on the overhead projector a cross section of a slave ship that showed little silhouetted figures lined up spoon-fashion. It was one of the most striking images I've ever seen; it just burned itself into my mind. I was beginning to write novels in 1970, and I actually wrote a version of *Middle Passage* in 1971. It was not successful because I was a young writer at the time, and I was telling it from the captain's point of view, so I couldn't get very close experientially to the slaves on the ship. So I put it aside and did six other books before I got back to it, but I accumulated more and more research on slavery and the slave trade over seventeen years.

The slave narrative is one of the most indigenous forms in American literature; it was born in this soil. It is related to the Puritan narrative, where someone would stand up in front of his community and talk about how he had gone from sin to salvation and found God. In slave narratives the movement is from a state of bondage to freedom. And if you take the Puritan narrative even further back to its origins, it will take you all the way to St. Augustine's *Confessions.*

So the literary background of the slave narrative, as well as its anchorage in the peculiar institution, slavery, made it very appealing to me as a form to work with. In *Oxherding Tale,* I wanted to unearth all those other forms and tell an adventure story at the same time. I wanted to make it a philosophical vehicle for late twentieth-century readers. I wanted to open it up to all of that richness of form and ideas that are already implicit in the slave narrative. I wanted to open up the question of bondage and liberation, not just in the Western context, but also in the Eastern context—bondage in a spiritual, in a sexual, in a metaphysical sense.

That was a very difficult book to do. It took five years and I threw out 2,400 pages. But it was the foundation for *Middle Passage* because we have a protagonist who speaks, sometimes, in a nineteenth-century kind of way, and who is in the white world and facing multiple dangers as he moves from bondage to liberation. In Rutherford's case, he's already a free man but he doesn't understand the meaning of freedom. He thinks it just means having the license to do whatever he wants to do. He doesn't realize that freedom involves responsibility on an individual and collective level.

DO: Of course, the Allmuseri whom Rutherford encounters on board the ship in the novel have a totally different sense of responsibility. Unlike him, or the sea captains in *Middle Passage* and *The Sea-Wolf,* they don't believe that people must necessarily be either predators or prey. What inspired you to create this tribe of Africans, who also appear in *Oxherding Tale* and *The Sorcerer's Apprentice,* as well as your most recent novel, *Dreamer?*

CJ: I've always been interested in different cultural interpretations of the world, different philosophical visions. Falcon's vision of the world is very dualistic. It is very "I versus Thou" as opposed to "I and Thou" or "I am Thou." If you look at the Allmuseri in the way I have developed them, there is a lot of Hinduism, Buddhism, and Taoism in their thought. What I wanted was a whole tribe of Gandhis and Mother Teresas. So I spent a lot of time in *Middle Passage* letting the Allmuseri come on stage in such a way that we would experience their culture through Rutherford, who is transformed by it by the end of the book.

There are people who ask me, when I do readings, if the All-museri still live in Africa; they think they are real. I wanted to create the most spiritual tribe imaginable—but the details themselves I didn't make up. The things I say about their language could equally be said about Mandarin Chinese. And the incident where the Allmuseri gave up one selfish desire in a special ceremony was done by a people in Kerala, India. Many of the details are actually taken from lots of so-called Third World cultures.

DO: Another fascinating parallel between *Middle Passage* and *Dreamer* is the way in which the story of Cain and Abel is played out in the two novels, between Rutherford and his brother Jackson in the former, and between Dr. Martin Luther King, Jr., and his double, Chaym, in the latter. How did this story come to have such resonance for you?

CJ: The story of Cain and Abel is actually a very short story—sixty lines in all—but it has permeated Western literature: the lines, "Am I my brother's keeper?" and "The voice of thy brother's blood cries out to Me from the ground"; the novels *Cane* and *East of Eden.* And

Cain is such a remarkable figure in his transformation over the past two thousand years.

But with *Dreamer* I wasn't thinking about Cain and Abel until the last of the seven years I worked on it; I had been wrestling with the idea of the doppelganger, or double. Then, at a conference, Dr. Ricardo Quinones handed me a book he had written that traces the Cain figure over the past two thousand years. It was pure serendipity, because I was scheduled to appear very shortly on a Bill Moyers television show about Cain and Abel. I still hadn't connected the dots to *Dreamer,* until my agent saw the show and suggested Cain as the double for King. Volumes of possibilities suddenly appeared before me, and I rewrote the entire novel from that angle; it provided the perfect structure that I needed. I think it had been in the back of my mind, and I just needed that interesting series of events to happen to bring it to inevitability.

The process of writing is an adventure; you never know how things are going to configure themselves. When I begin a book, I know it's going to transform my life. The characters may surprise me, the themes and the development of the themes may surprise me. They may even contradict some of my most cherished ideas, but that is appropriate. I really think the artist is more midwife, giving birth to this world, than anything else. If a writer isn't surprised and he doesn't feel suspense, then the reader won't.

DO: Toward the end of *Dreamer,* the character Martin Luther King, Jr., realizes that for him "the challenge of spirituality was simply this, to be good, truly moral and in control of oneself for this moment only because what other moment in time could a man be held responsible for?" In your view, what are the responsibilities of an artist trying to meet the challenge of spirituality?

CJ: I don't separate the intellectual life and the spiritual life and the creative life; they are all part of one life.

And yes, there is a tremendous social responsibility that comes with any public act we do, and that includes creative acts, as well.

First, one must satisfy oneself. You can't visualize for literary art a target audience the same way as you can for genre fiction; the audience for every book is unique.

But you have a moral responsibility to that audience to give them your best. There is a contract, I think, between the writer and the reader. As my old friend and teacher John Gardner used to say, You have to assume that your reader is as moral and as responsible and concerned about the world as yourself. He took a lot of heat for that. But I believe he is absolutely right, that fiction should be moral.

DO: And how do you define "moral"?

CJ: I define it much the way that he does. It's not moral in the sense that there are ideas or precepts that you preach at people; that is the opposite of moral. Moral is the process of the work itself, the creative process.

What do I mean by that? I mean that a work of art is moral when you give integrity to all of the principal characters. You don't set any of your characters up as straw men, or as foils, or as chess pieces; you give them all specific reasons for being the way they are, and then you follow and trace that. Even the objects in a fictional world are shot through with meaning and philosophical significance. So the moral fiction is a work of exploration, an intellectual adventure, an adventure of the spirit.

DO: And a philosophical adventure, as well, I would guess.

CJ: Oh, yes, absolutely. I think that a good work of fiction is comparable to a good work of philosophy. That means it must engage the life of the spirit as well as the life of the intellect. I don't want the characters to just talk the ideas; I want them grounded in the drama they find themselves in, in the world of action. Philosophy doesn't begin in some abstract realm; the questions that philosophers concern themselves with begin in human experience. When I write a novel, I want it to be a total work, a total performance.

BOOKS BY CHARLES JOHNSON
Black Humor
Half-Past Nation Time
Faith and the Good Thing
Oxherding Tale
The Sorcerer's Apprentice
Being and Race: Black Writing Since 1970
Middle Passage
Black Men Speaking (co-editor)
Africans in America: America's Journey through Slavery (co-author)
Dreamer
Soulcatcher and Other Stories
King: The Photobiography of Martin Luther King, Jr. (co-author)

Readers who want to learn more about Charles Johnson are encouraged to seek out some of the books that have shaped his writing life:
Moby-Dick and "Benito Cereno," Herman Melville
The Sea-Wolf, Jack London
Invisible Man, Ralph Ellison
Black Boy, Richard Wright
Cane, Jean Toomer
Siddhartha and *Steppenwolf*, Hermann Hesse
Grendel and *On Moral Fiction*, John Gardner
The Collected Short Stories, D. H. Lawrence
The Collected Works, Ralph Waldo Emerson
The Upanishads, *The Bhagavad-Gita*, and *The Dhammapada*

DIANE JOHNSON

Diane Johnson, a three-time Finalist for the National Book Award, in Fiction and Nonfiction, was born in Moline, Illinois, in 1934. A graduate of the University of Utah, she earned her M.A. and Ph.D. from the University of California, where she was a member of the faculty on the Davis campus for some twenty years, specializing in nineteenth-century literature. She earned her first National Book Award nomination in 1973 for Lesser Lives, *a biography of the first wife of British novelist George Meredith.* Lying Low, *a novel, was nominated for a National Book Award for Fiction in 1979, as was her critically ac-*

claimed bestseller Le Divorce, *in 1997. She has also been a Pulitzer Prize finalist twice, for* Terrorists and Novelists, *a collection of essays, and* Persian Nights, *a novel; and her biography,* Dashiell Hammett: A Life, *earned a* Los Angeles Times Book Prize *nomination in 1984. The author of four additional books, she also wrote the screenplay for Stanley Kubrick's unforgettable horror film* The Shining, *among others, and contributes essays and articles to a wide variety of magazines and journals, including* The New York Times, The New York Review of Books, *the* San Francisco Chronicle, *and* The Washington Post. *The recipient of honors, including a Mildred and Harold Strauss Living Award, she currently divides her time between Paris and San Francisco, where she lives with her husband, John Murray, a physician.*

In her brilliant comedy of manners Le Divorce, *Diane Johnson explores a theme that has absorbed her for much of her career: the endlessly surprising and occasionally dangerous ways in which men and women cope with cultural dislocation. Praised by The National Book Award's judges as a "subtle and serious examination of cross-Atlantic mores and morals,"* Le Divorce *illustrates that "European ideas about love and money and family obligation are sometimes disturbingly and even fatally different from our own."*

DIANE OSEN: You've said you were a bookish child whom everyone would take to the library. What did you read when you got there?

DIANE JOHNSON: The books I remember being very excited about as a child were by Alexandre Dumas and Raphael Sabatini—those and all the other books about going to sea that I could find, like *Two Years Before the Mast* and stories by Captain Marryat. I just systematically went along the library shelf reading them all. Sea stories and shipwrecks. I loved *Swiss Family Robinson*. I didn't like girls' stories, but I was absorbed by a bunch of boys and their parents having to make their own shelters when they're cast away on an island. I still love wonderful sea stories; I love Patrick O'Brian. I was quite old before I realized I myself, a Midwestern girl, wouldn't be going before the mast.

When I got a bit older, I started in on a list of one hundred great novels that I found somewhere. Often, I wouldn't get through them, because I was even so pretty young; and some of them the librarian wouldn't let me have, like *Madame Bovary*. But I remember reading *War and Peace* and *The Scarlet Letter* and so on.

DO: When did you first begin to write? And what was it that you wrote about?

DJ: The very first thing that I wrote I still have, and therefore can remember: It was a novel about thirty pages long, which I must have written when I was about nine or ten. It seems to have been very heavily influenced by the Bobbsey Twins books, because it has triplets—Dan, Don, and Dell, I think. Their parents have conveniently been lost—they have died in an airplane crash or something—so no adults impede them as they solve a mystery.

DO: Speaking of airplanes, I read recently that your ambition as a college freshman was to be a flight attendant. Is that true?

DJ: No. What I *did* say, because it's come back to haunt me, was that I went to a women's college that actually offered classes in how to be a flight attendant. At that time—this was in the fifties—it was considered quite a glamorous career for an adventurous young woman. My father was eager for me to be a flight attendant—he thought that would be a great thing to do—and so did I, but unfortunately I didn't grow to the requisite five foot six.

DO: That's interesting, because in a piece you wrote recently for *The New York Times* you paraphrased a friend who asserted that all fiction can be reduced to two plots: a stranger comes to town or someone goes on a trip. Most of your novels concern the latter, and feature characters who confront unfamiliar places, people, and circumstances. Why do you think this plot resonates so strongly with you?

DJ: I hadn't really thought about it, but your questions make me connect these issues: my childhood reading about adventure from a dull little town in the Midwest must have engendered or reflected some kind of wish to travel and go on adventures of my own. One of my first favorite books, which my father read to me, was called *Round the World with Bob and Betty*. Eventually I married someone who was also travel-minded, and whose job takes him into the far corners of the world; in this way I've had the opportunity to confront other cultures and places that otherwise I might not have. Lots of Midwesterners, I've noticed, have a sort of wanderlust—think of Hemingway, who grew up not too far from me. Above all, they want to get out of the Midwest and the safety and routine of Midwestern life.

The stranger going to a new place and feeling strange forms a plot, or a theme, in much of literature. And it must relate to what literature does, or why people read. I don't know if we know why people read, really, or want stories. But in much great literature we see people placed in taxing or unfamiliar circumstances, and in a vicarious way we understand our own responses; we plan on what we might do, and we allay our own anxieties about such experiences.

DO: Many of your narrators and main characters, from *Burning* and *Lying Low* to *Persian Nights* and *Le Divorce*, are women. Do you still believe, as you have said in the past, that female narrators are considered untrustworthy by many readers?

DJ: I do, and I'm happy that you touch on that, because I've always felt that people haven't been too interested in this observation. It's important to note that by "trustworthy" I mean in the sense of being a reliable narrator, that is, a narrator whose version of events can be believed by the reader. But I think that it's a really significant factor, in that the great heroines of literature are almost inevitably perceived—with some exceptions, [Jane Austen's] Elizabeth Bennett being one—as somehow unbalanced by either the dire circumstances that they're in, or by their being at an impressionable, romantic age. The corollary of that is that once they get to be older women, they are considered reliable. So if a grandmother is narrating a story, she's considered trustworthy, but the heroine who is vulnerable and of an age to fall in love is considered to be speaking from the heart, emotional, incapable of giving a true version of events, requiring the reader to see around or beyond her.

When I published *The Shadow Knows* I was very surprised when the heroine was taken for someone on the verge of paranoia—all kinds of pathologies were ascribed to her—when in fact she was just recounting, literally, what was happening: a dead cat on the doorstep, and so on. That was in no way meant to be the imaginings of an unbalanced mind. And then critics went on to say that her near-madness was because of her vulnerability or her motherhood or her circumstances, or because women are just like that—hysterical. At the time—and I guess this is what led me to my idea about the reliability of the female narrator—I thought, Well, if it were a man narrating this story, and he said there was a dead cat on the front step, would the reader believe him? And the answer is, almost certainly, Yes.

DO: Do you think reviewers and other readers are more open today to the notion that a young female narrator—like Isabel, for example, in *Le Divorce*—can actually have something credible to say?

DJ: Well, I think the novelist has to insist on the point that this is a trustworthy narrator. If not, she'll be considered a romantic heroine or whatever other category she falls into. I think the reader must be told rather blatantly that so-and-so is an intelligent, observant person.

Isabel, of course, is a first-person narrator, and a first-person narrator will never be seen as completely objective. My own procedure is always to have the first-person narrator focus on the other characters; thus she's cast in the role of observer/narrator, rather than a subjective experiencer of the narrative. Isabel sees her narrative task as to talk about Roxy and the Persand family and the others—whatever she's seeing. Once in a while, she'll mention her own feelings, but not enough, I think, to color the reader's perception of her as someone reliable; she's not so subjective that she becomes a victim/heroine and we have to cry with her.

DO: On the other hand, one of the pleasures of reading *Le Divorce* is recognizing just how often her judgments are wrong.

DJ: Well, Isabel has the perspective of a young narrator, and also of a stranger in a new culture. And that's what I wanted to do: have her misinterpret events, and say things that are naive, to bring to light the correct interpretation, which she eventually arrives at. She is reliable when looking back at her own misapprehensions.

DO: In terms of her background, Isabel is similar to many of your main characters—she's relatively young, as you said, fairly well-educated, and middle-class. What is it about characters of this age and these circumstances that continues to engage you?

DJ: It's not a matter of me being engaged by these factors so much as a reflection of the fact that the novel is by its nature a kind of middle-class form, at least in its classical formulation. The novel lends itself to cultural observations and nuances of manners, which require a certain cultural structure, usually middle-class.

But it's probably a limitation of my own background, too. I tend to write about the kind of people that I meet or out of my own experience, and that is rather limited. There are certainly novelists who can put themselves into other milieus and wonderfully capture them; but by and large, I think, the normal practice is to write about the kinds of people you know. That is what writers are advised to do. But I have been reproached, most recently in the English reviews of *Le Mariage*. They have gone out of their way to say, She only knows this rather elevated French milieu—which, I must say, was not my own perception, since I'm not French. I thought they were middle-class people much like us. Perhaps there would have been some kind of virtue in my getting to know the *charcutier* and writing about him, but I haven't had the opportunity.

DO: Isn't that maddening? Why should you write the book a reviewer wants you to write?

DJ: Why indeed? If people don't like books about middle-class people, if they are too tame, don't read them—but have a little pity on the poor novelist. I mean, when you think of all the classical novelists, the Midwesterners like Hemingway who *did* get down in the trenches with people, you find they have a kind of romantic condescension to all the bartenders and bullfighters they meet, condescension that we can today find rather irritating. Hemingway is still a middle-class boy wandering through Europe. But there is an assumption in American letters that a novel about the immigrant experience, or a regional novel, if set in an exotic region, is more authentic and realistic than, say, Indiana. I used to worry about that when I was young. I thought, How can I be a writer? I'm not Jewish, and I liked my parents, two hopeless drawbacks, two strikes against me. Ultimately, I think that one is just kind of stuck with one's own background and experience.

DO: Part of your background now is living and traveling a great deal outside the U.S., and writing about Americans abroad. What is it about the so-called international novel that intrigues you? And what did you mean when you said recently that you intended for *Le Divorce* to be a "reverse Jamesian novel"?

DJ: I guess I am intrigued by the same thing that drew me to adventure stories: going to other cultures, especially more worldly and exciting cultures than the one I was born into. Just as I was saying about Hemingway just now. As a writer you take with you the limitations of your background. As a reader, I've always been interested in issues of culture clash, whether it's a clash between the innocent and the knowing, the modern and the old-fashioned, or the life-affirming and the life-denying. A Jamesian novel often revolves around a raw Yank coming over to Europe, or a kind of violated innocent who learns things from the wily Europeans. In *Le Divorce* I was playing with the idea that that formulation might, in some respects, be reversed now that it is apt to be Europeans who cling to traditions and families and even to their religions, and can seem naive. They're letting the wily Americans seduce them with a cultural imperialism that they, for some reason, don't resist, in the same way none of the Americans in James resist European culture.

As a writer, of course I have always been drawn to James's skill at writing novels; his critical pronouncements about such things as point of view have affected me very much. And I've always been impressed by the way in which he earns high moral seriousness in novels with rather lurid situations. For instance, in *The Wings of the Dove* you have fraud, death, fornication, and so on, but he foregrounds the moral issues in a way I admire—it's interesting and kind of naughty. He's sort of a scamp (dare one say?) in putting over all this high seriousness with no·sacrifice of low excitement.

What I also love about James is his prefaces; they are filled with pearls of wisdom and instruction for anyone who is trying to write a novel. I read them all the time, and even constructed an index for them, because the first copy of *The Art of the Novel* that I bought didn't have one. He's very interesting even if you don't agree with him. For instance, I don't agree that you always have to use the limited consciousness of one character, but nonetheless he has good reasons for the things he does, and he explains them in a way that few writers do.

If I could just add, lately I've been reading a lot of Anthony Trollope, and in a way he's so much more lovable and enjoyable than James, and he has quite a lot of high moral seriousness as well. I just reread the Palliser novels, and was looking at how Trollope has the characters come from one book into another—and it's so impressive. He's a very underrated writer; I think that he actually sunk his own reputation by revealing that he wrote all those pages before breakfast. His writing was probably a compulsion, but he made himself seem like a hack; if he had presented himself as a man driven to write before he had to go to his workaday toil, posterity would have revered him much more. And if James had been more like Trollope, he would have been even greater.

DO: Many critics and readers have compared *Le Divorce* with *Pride and Prejudice*, which is in fact one of your favorite novels. When did you encounter it? And how did your understanding of Austen's intentions for the novel change over the years?

DJ: When I was a teenager I thought of *Pride and Prejudice* simply as the heart-stopping story of Elizabeth Bennett. Will she get married? What will happen to her sisters? As I became more familiar with the condition of women at that time, with the precariousness of their social and economic position, I began to see that Austen was writing about the whole moral structure of her society. The serious aspects of the novel were much clearer to me.

You know, all writers have tricks to get themselves going; and one of mine is to find a book that can become the inspiration for the book *I'm* writing, not in terms of its plot or characters, but because of its structure or some other formal detail. For instance, when I was writing *The Shadow Knows,* I outlined *The Good Soldier,* because I wanted to see how Ford Madox Ford foreshadows in one chapter the things that happen in the next. Years later, at different times, I outlined both *Pride and Prejudice* and *Emma,* to try to see how they are divided into acts and how Austen manages the progression of the various characters—and I was more dazzled than ever by her great genius. I was especially fascinated by her brilliance as a comic novelist, by how she skillfully mixes more broadly comic characters with the nuanced main characters. It also emerged that those novels have a much more powerful structure than one might imagine. *Pride and Prejudice,* for instance, has five acts and features very classical reversals and subplots that are introduced at the appropriate times in the appropriate acts. Either she had a very powerfully organized mind, or she made an outline herself. I don't know if anyone has ever found any working materials from Jane Austen, but it wouldn't have been like her to keep them, anyway.

DO: To what degree did *Pride and Prejudice* perhaps inspire you to write your own novel about a pair of sisters with opposing sensibilities?

DJ: An allusion to *Pride and Prejudice* wasn't altogether conscious. I really had the Roxy story in mind—the ubiquitous story of the American woman who marries a French man, and then he leaves and she stays in France. I thought that was interesting, and I had an actual model in mind, a friend who is a sort of Roxy. But then I needed a speaker and I arrived at Isabel, whose voice is like mine, grafted onto my daughters' voices and so on, in the way one combines people one knows. At the beginning she was not the focus of the book, and she does not believe that she is the focus; she believes she is the agent telling the story of Roxy. But then, of course, the other characters got interested in Isabel, and so did I.

DO: What about another one of your favorite books, Angus Wilson's *Anglo-Saxon Attitudes?* How did you discover that novel, and how did reading it affect your own approach to writing?

DJ: I remember very clearly what it meant to me at the time that I read it initially. [The novelist] Alison Lurie is a great friend of mine; when we met I was twenty-one or so and living in Los Angeles, and Alison was married to a member of the "Eastern literary establishment." She had access to a whole world that I had never even heard of, let alone knew anything about. We became friends and she recommended things for me to read—she read books that were fashionable in Anglophile literary circles—and she gave me *Anglo-Saxon Attitudes.* I was just thrilled by it, especially by the worldly facetiousness of its tone, which I thought was just so unbelievably sophisticated.

Rereading it recently, I was put off by that very thing at first; but when I got used to it I admired the book all over again for the brilliance and complexity of the way in which Wilson presents the whole family. The wife, the husband, the daughter with the withered hand—they are all so vividly etched on my imagination. I think it may even help me in a book I'm writing now, about different attitudes toward inheritance. I think I can use the rhythm with which Wilson brings in each of the family characters, and unifies them with the character of Gerald, the father, who has his own memories. It's actually not unlike what I'm doing with this new novel, except that the Gerald character is a woman, long resident in France, in her early sixties, with at least one daughter; so finding *Anglo-Saxon Attitudes* again was a delicious serendipity.

DO: Are you also planning to interweave the past and the present, as Wilson does?

DJ: No, I don't think so. I remember once, when I was a graduate student at UCLA, Christopher Isherwood came as Regents professor, and his job was to read student manuscripts. When he read mine, he said, disapprovingly, You need to ground everyone in their pasts with their childhood traumas and the objective correlatives— and you haven't done that. And I think my heart hardened at that moment about having to do that. So I never have, or not much, still defying Isherwood.

DO: We spoke earlier about Trollope's skill at bringing characters from one book into another, which is something you do as well in *Le Divorce* and *Le Mariage*. Will we find any familiar characters in your new novel?

DJ: Well, I've recently discovered that when people buy film rights to a book, they also buy the rights to the characters—and you have to get their permission to bring those characters back. So I may actually have been in violation when I brought back Antoine and his mother in *Le Mariage,* but nobody so far has objected.

For this new book I'm trying to work in a little walk-on part for Isabel, and maybe for a couple of others as well, but I'm not sure whether I've signed the characters away forever. And I've just realized that one of my heroines, Amy, may be a recurrent character from a very old book of mine. In my mind she has always been a lawyer, but now she is a lawyer who has made unforeseen millions in the dot-com world, and has come to France for self-improvement because she realizes she doesn't know anything. That came about from a chance, overheard remark in an antique shop in Seattle, where the dealer was denouncing her young, dot-com customers. She said, If it weren't for Martha Stewart they wouldn't even know that they have to iron their tablecloths. That enriched my understanding of Amy, and it's something that happens rather often, at least to me: I sort of thrash around in the beginning and then I realize something about a character that I did not know at first. There are writers who know everything about their characters before they start, and that's, I'm sure, the better way. But alas, that's something I've never been able to do.

DO: You live in France now, too. How has your decision to divide your time between Paris and San Francisco affected writing life?

DJ: I have always written about where I am or where I have just been. I spend less and less time in San Francisco—maybe three or four months in the summer—but it's not really my decision so much as my husband's. John works for a nonprofit agency based in France that works against tuberculosis and AIDS in Africa.

But it is easier for me to write here, because it's slightly easier to live in France than in San Francisco, for many reasons. One of them is that you don't have to have a car in Paris. I know this doesn't mean anything to a New Yorker, but anybody else in America will appreciate the difference: you can save hours every day. And then one of our kids married a Frenchman, giving me this French family, which is a great bonus to a novelist.

DO: Are you still writing nonfiction as well as novels?

DJ: In a desultory fashion, I'm working on another book like *Natural Opium*. Whether that was a book of essays or stories was never quite decided—some of the pieces were later republished in essay collections, and some in short-story collections. And I thought that was a very revealing statement about this kind of mixed genre that I find myself working in, where the stories are all true, but the dates and names may have been changed, or different events, a year or two apart, conflated into one trip. There's a little formal tampering with an essentially true narrative. Truth or fiction is, after all, only a matter of degree—a novel is also nonfiction and fiction, real but altered, and sometimes only very transparently.

My new book is a kind of memoir called *Men on Top,* or maybe *Leading Men,* because it's about various categories of male authority figure. I've already published two pieces, about generals and sheiks. Some of the others will be about directors, because I've worked with all these directors—I've written one screenplay apiece for Stanley Kubrick, Sidney Pollack, Mike Nichols, and Francis Coppola—and I find them very interesting. Maybe doctors. Uncles! Loggers!

DO: I jotted down the names of some of the authors whose books Isabel reads in *Le Divorce* in an effort, as she puts it, to "break through to seriousness": Breton, Sartre, de Tocqueville, Bilge Karasu. Similarly, Ann-Sophie in *Le Mariage* regularly turns to books for guidance in her daily life. What do you hope readers will take away from your books?

DJ: I guess I would like them to take away the idea of other cultures being as valuable or even possibly in some ways superior to our own—the idea of cultural perspective. This is an idea, I think, that Americans lack totally, because we're not trained to think that any other cultures could have value, and we assume that they all want to be like us.

I would also like them to take away the idea of the seriousness of the comic novel. I hate reviews that just say, Oh, it was so funny, when, of course, I meant something serious, too. You couldn't really write a novel unless you meant it. What would be the point? I think there is a kind of secret didacticism to novel writing, and I have as much as anyone this didactic streak. Maybe worse.

BOOKS BY DIANE JOHNSON

FICTION
Fair Game
Loving Hands at Home
Burning
The Shadow Knows
Lying Low
Persian Nights
Health and Happiness
Le Divorce
Le Mariage

NONFICTION
Lesser Lives
Dashiell Hammett
Terrorists and Novelists
Natural Opium

Readers who want to learn more about Diane Johnson are encouraged to read some of the books that have shaped her life as a writer:

Pride and Prejudice, Jane Austen
Anglo-Saxon Attitudes, Angus Wilson
Love and Friendship, Alison Lurie
The Three Musketeers and *The Count of Monte Cristo,* Alexandre Dumas
The Story Girl, L. M. Montgomery
Two Years Before the Mast, Richard Henry Dana, Jr.
USA, John Dos Passos
The Great Gatsby, F. Scott Fitzgerald
A House in Order, Nigel Dennis
The Bell, Iris Murdoch
The Leopard, Guiseppe di Lampedusa

PHILIP LEVINE

Born in Detroit, Michigan, on January 10, 1928, two-time National Book Award Winner Philip Levine first began composing poetry at the age of fourteen, inspired by the flowering of a mock orange bush purchased with money he had earned washing windows. "I looked on the work my hands had wrought," he recalled later, "then I said in my heart, As it happened to the gardener so it happened to me, for we all go into one place; we are all earth and return to earth. The dark was everywhere, and as my voice went out I was sure it reached the edges of creation."

By the age of eighteen he was writing seriously, as a student at Wayne State University, and while working at a succession of monot-

onous, backbreaking and dangerous jobs at factories in Detroit. In 1954 he married Frances Artley and soon began teaching at the University of Iowa, earning an MFA before joining the faculty of California State University in Fresno in 1958.

Since then, he has published more than twenty books of poems, including Ashes, *which won the 1979 National Book Award for Poetry, and* What Work Is, *which won the National Book Award for Poetry twelve years later; his collection* The Simple Truth *won the Pulitzer Prize in 1995. A member of The American Academy of Arts and Letters, Mr. Levine is also the recipient of honors including the Ruth Lilly Award, the National Book Critics Circle Prize, the Frank O'Hara Prize, and the Levinson Prize. He continues to write poetry, he once explained, "for people for whom there is no poetry ... the people I grew up with who brothered, sistered, fathered, and mothered me, and lived and worked beside me. Their presence seemed utterly lacking in the poetry I inherited at age twenty, so I've spent the last forty-some years trying to add to our poetry what wasn't there."*

DIANE OSEN: When did you first discover poetry?

PHILIP LEVINE: As a child I lived in a house that was rather tumultuous. My father died when I was five. My mother, who worked full-time, raised us; I had two brothers. My grandfather lived only a few blocks away, and he would come over quite often. Somebody had to make dinner, somebody had to do the dishes, and arguments started.

In order to relieve myself from the burdens of family wars, I would go out. I was fortunate at that moment in my life to be living on the outskirts of Detroit, where my mother had bought a house when I was twelve. When we entered World War II there was a freeze on housing, so there was an enormous area around us with no houses whatsoever. I would walk through these undeveloped blocks, which were thick with trees, just to get rid of the noise of the house.

And at some point, at age fourteen, I began to speak what I could only call poems, probably bad poems. They were not based on the poems that I was reading in school, which either overwhelmed me, like *The Canterbury Tales,* or bored me stiff, like nineteenth-century American and British nature poetry, which seemed too genteel and irrelevant. But there was a source for the cadences that I was using. And that source was a curious one: the cadences of the Southern preachers, both black and white, that I heard on the radio on Sunday mornings. I was absolutely thrilled by the way they used language.

I would begin speaking these poems—which had very simple subjects, like the odor of the earth when it's rained on, or the majesty of the trees—and I would get a kind of rolling gait going. I would say things like, "The rain falling on my hands today falls on the hands of people in China and Uruguay. The rain that is a gift to me is a gift from eternity. The rain that is caressing your face will caress your face for as long as you live." The poetry had a movement like that. I hadn't read Whitman yet so I can't say it was Whitmanesque, but Whitman based some of his cadences on religious oratory as well.

I never wrote these poems down. I think my hesitancy had to do with the fact that I was a twin, and was afraid that my brother would find them and taunt me mercilessly, and probably show them to our classmates. There were perhaps a dozen poems that I memorized and honed and recited and revised. And they were a great satisfaction to me, because they gave me an avenue to speak in a world in which I had not discovered any other avenue to say the things that I needed to say. I went on with this activity for about two years. My guess is that I stopped because I got interested in girls. And getting interested in girls—women under the age of eighteen were called girls then—was a whole enterprise.

I began, you might say, my second career as a poet through the agency of a high school teacher who read us the poem "Arms and the Boy," by Wilfred Owen. Now, by this time it was 1944, and I was waiting to finish high school and be drafted into the service. The fear of war was something we never spoke about; I never even spoke about it with my twin brother. The public presentation of young men with that kind of fear was awful. In the movies, for example, they were portrayed as almost wicked in their unwillingness to die for their country.

In *The Collected Poems* of Wilfred Owen, I discovered a young Englishman who had indeed died for his country—but who shared my fears, and in a way authenticated them. Reading Owen, I realized I was not only moved by the power of the poetry, but by something happening within myself—that I could say of myself, I'm not abnormal. This reaction that I was having was a normal human reaction to war: I didn't want to be killed and I didn't want to kill anybody. It would have been abnormal for me to do what my classmate, Johnny Moradian, had done: enlist in the service, go off and get killed. And that started me off on my second career.

DO: What else were you reading then that you especially enjoyed?

PL: Before I started college, most of the books I read I found in the house. My mother and my father had been avid readers, and their focus had been nineteenth-century Russian and French fiction; so I was reading Balzac and Chekhov and Dostoevsky. I also loved plays, as my mother did. When I was young, it seemed as though I could read a play and almost do it in my head. Chekhov, Gorky, and O'Neill were probably my three favorite playwrights. Clifford Odets was just as important back then, too, because his politics were so clearly announced, and he led me right to Arthur Miller.

It was in my first year of college that I began to discover fiction written in English, by people like John Dos Passos and Theodore Dreiser. Another writer who absolutely overwhelmed me was Virginia Woolf. The only weakness of Dos Passos, it seemed then to me, was that he didn't pry deeply enough into the nature of his characters; whereas with Woolf, I felt she was going right to the bottom of these people, and that she loved them with an enormous power.

I was probably twenty or twenty-one when I took a year-long course at Wayne State University, from Vera Sandamosky Dunham, in Dostoevsky and Tolstoy; and it was in that class that I read *The Cossacks*. I must say, rereading it last week I was surprised by it.

DO: What were you surprised by?

PL: Well, it wasn't the book that I thought I'd read. I think I had added things to it that weren't there and probably subtracted things, too. Of course, that was fifty years ago and I wasn't aware of how much class functioned in it. I didn't see Olenin as a type—a type of rich young man whose early life is given to getting into debt and fooling around until he departs from that and decides, I will not be that guy, I will try to become someone else. I didn't know to what degree that was a bold step.

I also didn't see that there was a certain amount of condescension, almost wonderment, in Tolstoy, that these uncivilized Cossacks could have something to teach a gentleman. At the time that I was reading the book, I was living and working with ordinary people from God knows where—Ireland, Hungary, Russia, the American South—who, it seemed to me, had a good deal to teach me about the world. So there was a way in which this book was telling me, Keep your eyes open, you'll learn a lot from the people around you, just as Olenin learns a hell of a lot about life from the people around him.

Rereading *The Cossacks,* the character who impressed me the most was Marianka—her resilience, and her extraordinary appetite for life, and her willingness to choose against the will of her parents, who clearly want her to choose Olenin because he's somebody who can advance their family. But she sees in Luka finally a kind of natural nobleman—a superior man. Another thing that surprised me—that in this book, and in "Happily Ever After" and "The Death of Ivan Ilyich," I found Tolstoy demeaning women. Also, as a reader in 1999, I was shocked that there was no overt sexuality.

DO: Were you also struck, as I was, by how often the characters talk about self-sacrifice, and whether it's the key to living rightly?

PL: I was struck by it and appalled by it. It's something that I was used to in Dostoevsky—that there is a sort of Christian calling that requires a life lived for others. But in Tolstoy—and I think this makes him a richer writer—there's always a struggle going on. The characters are always talking greatly about sacrifice, which I take to be part of their education as Christians. At the same time, there is this volcanic urge to reach out and embrace the riches of the world, which has nothing to do with sacrifice; it has to do with taking what's here and feeding it into the self so the self can grow. I feel this struggle going on always in all three of these stories—the struggle between the taught ethic and the natural instinct. And I feel that Tolstoy himself is torn between these two.

Yet again and again and again in my reading I came across scenes of such urgent vitality, such beautiful, full responses to the glory of the natural world and to people going about their daily lives. I was, at times, just wowed by how gorgeously he wrote. He still feels like a very great writer to me.

DO: More people than ever have probably heard of Walt Whitman today, thanks to President Clinton's interest in *Leaves of Grass.* When did you first discover him? And what was it about his poetry that you responded to most strongly?

PL: I didn't take him as seriously as I should until I was twenty-six years old. I say that with a certain amount of shame; I should have seen how strong he was before. But I was reading the wrong poems and seeing only his optimism about progress—that rubbed me the wrong way. When I finally settled on "Song of Myself" I saw how great he was.

"Song of Myself" pushes in a variety of directions, but the vision that moved me most was, "I am you. We are one creation." I believed it even before I read it. And also, "There is that lot of me and all so luscious." The bravery of such a line, the claim: I am unique but I am unique in the way that you are also unique, because each of us is a little cosmos and one is as good as another. I was just thunderstruck by that notion, because one is constantly being told, You're ordinary. And Whitman is saying, Yes, you are ordinary, because the ordinary is the storehouse of the extraordinary; the only place you're ever going to encounter the extraordinary is going to be in the ordinary, in the daily. And the frank embrace of the sensual and the self; what a rewarding way to see ourselves.

DO: Of course, many of your poems also find transcendence in the ordinary, particularly in *What Work Is*. What can you say about the origins of two of my favorite poems from that collection, "Fear and Fame" and "Every Blessed Day"?

PL: There is a good deal of invention in the book, but "Fear and Fame" is one of the few poems in which I really am trying to capture an experience that was mine. It is based on a job that I had for a year at a plumbing concern that chrome-plated pipes and other things. I was given the job of preparing the chemical baths that were used in the plating process, and I put on all of this equipment so that I wouldn't get burned. And even then, sometimes I'd go home at night and discover that, for example, a shirt might be almost reduced to lace because some of the acid had gotten through. I was regarded with a kind of awe by the people I worked with, because almost no one else wanted to do this. They were scared. But there was something lovely about the job because I worked utterly alone. It was a very peaceful job. And once I learned how to do it and got over my fear of it, it became automatic and my mind was released to go where it might.

One day at the lunch break, a cake was produced and everyone sang "Happy Birthday" to me. I said, It's not my birthday, and they said, No, but you've been here exactly a year. And the next day I quit, because it seemed as though only a few months had passed and I thought the rest of my life could pass in the same way if I didn't get out of there.

DO: What about "Every Blessed Day"?

PL: Something enters this poem that, of course, doesn't enter the other poem, and that's my father. The stories that my father told me as a child I still remember, even though he died when I was five. He was in the First World War, in the British Army. He was an officer stationed in what was then called Palestine, in charge of a camp for Turkish prisoners. He finally deserted because he couldn't stand it. But in his stories the desert was like magic; it enthralled and entranced him.

Here I guess I'm describing myself as a twenty-five- or twenty-six-year-old guy, already through college, living rather badly, getting up in the dark to go to work. In a few minutes this man in the poem will hold his time card over the time clock. He can drop it in—the clock made a noise, ka-chump—or he can not. But no matter what his decision is, the day will go on being the day; his decision has no meaning for anybody except himself. And realizing this, he lets the card fall and he accepts his fate.

There's an irony here, because I'm not my father's son: He was an adventurer, a much more independent man. And I'm feeling, in this poem, that I have let him down, that if I had measured up to him, I would not have dropped that card. On the other hand, I've accepted my life and in that way the day has a certain blessedness to it, although I haven't gotten the full measure of that blessedness.

"What Work Is" is also a poem based on a real experience, but all the material that deals with my brother is made up. At this time, I was married unhappily [to my first wife] and I went to apply for a job at the Ford Highland Park factory. The newspaper said to be there at eight. I got there on time and there were a great many guys standing in front of me; the employment office didn't open till ten. As I stood out there in the light rain, I figured out that it was a test: If you were willing to stand two hours in the rain then you were the guy they wanted. You were a born serf. I didn't get the job, but somehow I remembered that day and this poem came out of that experience.

It also came out of another experience. My brother by this time was married. I didn't see him as much as I would have liked and I was constantly seeing his face in other guys' faces. That got into the poem, too, and then it became a poem about brothers, really. So it took off from one experience but it really is about a different experience.

DO: You described yourself, in a recent interview, as a poet of memory. What did you mean? And how do your experiences—and those of your family—influence your work today?

PL: Curiously, it's a fairly recent phenomenon. If you went back and looked at my earlier work, you would see that there weren't that many poems of memory up until maybe twenty years ago—and then there are an enormous number. I believe it comes out of being a father. I sit with my children—I'm very close to my sons—and they love to talk about the past. They ask me all kinds of questions and I'm happy to tell them what I know. But when they talk about our lives together, they get everything wrong—according to me. I seldom correct them, but I've come to realize that each of us carries a mythology of what took place. The truths are much more complex.

Coleridge remarked that the only material the imagination has to work on is the material of memory. I think that's true. You deal with it in different ways; you recombine it, you invent a great deal, using remembered elements. Poets are supposed to invent.

DO: How has the form of your poems changed over time?

PL: For many years I worked in a much shorter line, because I liked the kind of rhythmic drive that the short line can give when it runs over. But at a certain point I wanted more details—a larger, fuller sense of place. I wanted to be more Tolstoyan, let's say, and for that I had to use a longer line. I'm not writing as much for the rhythmic drive now; I'm much more concerned with the objects and the people and the feel of the places. And the poems are more meditative, calmer.

DO: You were a professor at Fresno State University for more than twenty years, and even though you've retired, you still teach. Was it difficult to balance the demands of an academic career with the demands of your writing life?

PL: The answer would be, Yes, especially at first, because I taught too much and it drained a lot of energy from me. By the time I was in my early forties I realized, through my wife's insight, that I was my best student—that in trying to excite young people about literature, the person who got the most excited was I. So in the long run it has been a good thing to have two careers that seem worthy to me, and that you can never get too good at. You can never be too good a teacher; you can never be too good a poet.

DO: Have the reasons you write poetry changed much over the course of your career? And what about your sense of a poet's responsibilities toward his or her readers?

PL: If you looked at my writing life, you would see that up until I'm forty-five, I don't even seem to have readers, or very few. Then things happen, and I become somebody who is talked about and read, and I meet my readers. So my attitude towards the reader changed a great deal.

I think my original notion of the reader was someone doing his best not to have an intense emotional experience, and I needed somehow to sneak under the locked door and surprise him. I think that attitude is still there. My later experience with the reader is that he and she like what I'm doing. They're glad that there is a person with my sensibility.

I can't speak for other writers, but I know that any responsibilities to the reader don't concern me when I'm actually writing; later, when I feel the poem is as good as it'll get, I feel obliged not to burden my readers with the garbage I write. Like everyone else who writes, I write badly at times, and I try never to publish the junk. I'd have to say I write because it pleases me to do so. Well, it's more than that: I would feel incomplete without it. I do it out of the joy of doing it. Not that it isn't awful work much of the time, but when you do it right it's glorious and I feel then that whatever I write has to be true. My obligation is more to the poem than the reader. I'm sorry if the reader doesn't like it, but it's what I felt I had to write. I

feel like the sparrow in the great William Carlos Williams poem: I
did my best.

BOOKS BY PHILIP LEVINE
> *On the Edge*
> *Not This Pig*
> *Pili's Wall*
> *Red Dust*
> *They Feed They Lion*
> *1933*
> *The Names of the Lost*
> *Ashes: Poems New and Old*
> *7 Years from Somewhere*
> *Don't Ask* (interviews)
> *One for the Rose*
> *Selected Poems*
> *Sweet Will*
> *A Walk with Tom Jefferson*
> *New Selected Poems*
> *What Work Is*
> *The Bread of Time* (essays)
> *The Simple Truth*
> *Unselected Poems*
> *The Mercy*

Readers who want to learn more about Philip Levine are encouraged to
seek out some of the books that have shaped his writing life:
> "Song of Myself," Walt Whitman
> *The Collected Poems,* Wilfred Owen
> *Hard Labor,* Cesare Pavese
> *Poet in New York,* Federico García Lorca
> *Spring and All* and *In the American Grain,* William Carlos Williams
> *The Collected Poems,* Emily Dickinson
> *The Canterbury Tales,* Geoffrey Chaucer
> *The Poems* and *The Selected Letters,* John Keats
> *Hamlet* and *The Tempest,* William Shakespeare
> *War and Peace,* Leo Tolstoy
> *Mrs. Dalloway,* Virginia Woolf

USA, John Dos Passos

Sister Carrie, Theodore Dreiser

Southern Road, Sterling Brown

Winesburg, Ohio, Sherwood Anderson

The Great Gatsby, F. Scott Fitzgerald

Studies in Classic American Literature, D. H. Lawrence

In Defense of Reason, Yvor Winters

The Road Back to Paris and *The Sweet Science,* A. J. Liebling

Homage to Catalonia and *Shooting an Elephant,* George Orwell

The Collected Stories and *A Farewell to Arms,* Ernest Hemingway

The Collected Poems, Dylan Thomas

Death on the Installment Plan, Louis-Ferdinand Céline

Residence on Earth, Pablo Neruda

The Collected Poems, Thomas Hardy

Poems, Ben Jonson

Postwar Polish Poetry, Czeslaw Milosz (editor)

Harmonium, Wallace Stevens

The Neon Wilderness, Nelson Algren

The Lyrical Ballads, Samuel Taylor Coleridge and William Words-
    worth

Letters to a Young Poet, Rainer Maria Rilke

Invisible Man, Ralph Ellison

Roots and Wings, Hardie St. Martin (editor)

Ha! Ha! Among the Trumpets, Alun Lewis

DAVID LEVERING LEWIS

David Levering Lewis, a two-time Finalist for the National Book Award for his biographies W.E.B. Du Bois: Biography of a Race, 1868–1919 *(1994) and* W.E.B. Du Bois: The Fight for Equality and the American Century, 1919–1963 *(2000), was born in Little Rock, Arkansas, in 1936, and grew up in Wilberforce, Ohio. His mother was a teacher, his father a high school principal in Little Rock*

who sacrificed his job over his insistence that African-American teachers receive salaries equal to those of their white counterparts. After his father was appointed president of Morris Brown College in Atlanta, Dr. Lewis enrolled in Booker T. Washington High School, the same high school that Martin Luther King, Jr., had attended a few years earlier; like him, Dr. Lewis left the school early, in his case to participate in the Ford Foundation–sponsored Early Entrants Program at Fisk University, from which he graduated in 1956. After attending the University of Michigan Law School for one semester, he entered the graduate history department at Columbia University, where he earned a master's degree in 1958. He earned his Ph.D. from the London School of Economics in 1962, having studied Modern European and French history. Following a stint as a lecturer at the University of Ghana, Lewis returned to the United States, serving on the faculties of Morgan State University in Baltimore, the University of the District of Columbia, and the University of California at San Diego. In 1985, he was appointed to the Martin Luther King, Jr., chair at Rutgers, the state university of New Jersey.

In addition to his teaching and research, Professor Lewis is the author of numerous scholarly articles reflecting his interest in comparative history, as well as seven books, including King: A Critical Biography, Prisoners of Honor: The Dreyfus Affair, *and* The Race to Fashoda: European Colonialism and African Resistance in the Scramble for Africa. *The first volume of his biography of Du Bois won the 1994 Pulitzer Prize in Biography, the National Conference of Black Political Scientists Outstanding Book Award, the Bancroft Prize in American History and Diplomacy, and the Phi Beta Kappa Award, among others. The second volume also won the Pulitzer Prize in 2001. A founding member of the Committee for Policy on Racial Justice and a member of the American Historical Association, he is the father of four children and lives in New York City with his wife, Ruth Ann Stewart.*

DIANE OSEN: As the son of an educator and a college president, you were raised in a home where books and scholarship were treasured. Did you share your parents' interest in reading and writing as a child, or did it take a bit longer to emerge?

DAVID LEVERING LEWIS: I think it emerged very early on. Among my earliest memories is my father's study in Ohio. You could enter the home through a front door that led into the parlor, or a side door that led to my father's study. I usually entered and exited through his study, and so I passed through books always. I remember particularly a series of large leather-bound volumes of world history which, I suspect, had been written by a German historian and translated into English. The collection began with Egypt and came forward to the period just after World War I, and it was wonderfully illustrated. I spent a lot of time with those pictures, and I was probably bitten by the history bug before the onset of my teens.

DO: I know from having read the first volume of your biography about W.E.B. Du Bois that he, too, was bitten by the history bug at an early age, and that reading Macaulay's *History of England* had an enormous impact on both his choice of profession and his writing life. Did you experience a similar epiphany?

DLL: When I was in high school, Will and Ariel Durant had a very, very deep impact on me. I haven't gone back and read their books in many years—and I probably don't want to, because I don't want to risk disappointment—but at that time in my life I found the narrative drive of the Durants marvelous. I admired their ability to take chunks of history and make great sense of not only the personalities, but also the forces, at work. Of course, I learned very quickly in college, and certainly in graduate school, to pooh-pooh the Durants as popularizers of history who in fact missed the truly deep forces at work, or who simplified them. That's probably true, but I wasn't looking for a graduate seminar then. Emil Ludwig's biographies of Martin Luther and Napoleon and Julius Caesar also left a great imprint and eventually flavored my own writing.

I must admit that I never have been much of a fiction reader. My mother read to me just about every child's story that was in the canon, and I remember her saying to me that she was never able to read the same story over again, because I didn't want to hear it twice; I just liked to get the sense of it and move on. I regret that now, particularly because I think reading good fiction is helpful when one wants to write well—and I might have written well with less effort if I had read more fiction.

DO: As you of course know, there are many parallels between your early career in academia and Du Bois's: You both studied history; you both graduated from Fisk University and did doctoral work abroad; and you both lived in and wrote about Africa. Thanks to your biography, I know some of the reasons behind the choices Du Bois made; what were some of the factors that influenced *your* choices?

DLL: Not remaining in law school was one of the most important factors. I was at a very good law school for one semester and did well enough, but it was clear to me that I didn't want law for a career. So I jumped ship—literally—by hopping on board a bus to New York and petitioning the dean of Columbia University, Jacques Barzun, for special admission into the history program and a stipend. Had I known how inappropriate that was, I wouldn't have done it.

Although I took a master's degree in U.S. history, what I wanted was to do European history, which is why I did not continue my graduate studies in this country. The lure of London and Paris was very great at a time when the cost of a comparable education abroad was one-third or less than in the United States. And at the time, I didn't realize how rich our own history is; I thought it was a pretty clear story of a tax revolt and a civil war, followed by a lot of industrial and commercial dynamism. On the other hand, I found French history utterly fascinating, and I found living in France a reinforcement of the fascination. And then, being a person of color, there were concerns I had about civil rights that many people in U.S. graduate schools in those years may not have sensed, and France was a place where, for an expatriate American, concerns about civil rights were academic, if they existed at all. So when I was able to go to Africa to teach at the university level, the prospect just seemed to me irresistible. I thought—as had Du Bois, who expired three months before I arrived in Ghana—that Africa was going to be one of the most exciting places on the planet, and that it would be a wonderful thing to be connected with that effervescence and historical change. But after a year I found myself back in the United States, and my career path then took a different trajectory.

DO: What you said just now about your concerns vis-à-vis civil rights reminded me of something you mentioned once to another interviewer: that Du Bois was someone who was discussed at the dinner table while you were growing up. What did you and your family think of him then, and when did you encounter *The Souls of Black Folk,* the book that propelled him to fame, and one that eventually changed your life, as well?

DLL: I don't know that I can be terribly vivid in my recollections, but I can say that my family exemplified in some ways the split between the tradition of Booker T. Washington and the tradition of W.E.B. Du Bois. My father was much more accommodating to the tensions between the two traditions; as a college president, he naturally was a pretty practical man. My mother, though, was a resolute Du Boisian, and I think it would be fair to say that whenever the name Booker Washington was mentioned she would sort of blanch; she thought that his take on race relations and civil rights was a great mistake. These family prejudices meant that the people in our social circle tended to be typical of those whom Du Bois characterized as the "Talented Tenth"—professional people with a certain degree of affluence and a great sense of racial purpose who believed that the advantages they had attained brought with them obligations of social service and principled conduct. So sometimes the atmosphere was a little stuffy and dinner conversations were like the discussions I imagined one might hear at the State Department.

The Souls of Black Folk must have been in the air at our home; my knowledge of it came early on. My mother wrote plays that were performed by her students, and passages from *The Souls of Black Folk* were invoked ofttimes—passages about double consciousness, and the famous tag line about the color line and the twentieth century. I don't remember the first time I read the book, but I know it couldn't have been early in elementary school, because I couldn't read until I was about nine years old; that's why those children's stories were read to me by my mother. Eventually the reading impairment vanished as though it had never existed, and once that nonreading fog lifted, there I was with these stories in my head.

The Souls of Black Folk became important to me because it is one of the most important books in the American canon. I found it beautifully written and still find it so, but I have to say that today's students sometimes puzzle over the circumlocutory phrasings. But I find the language as vivid today as when I was first exposed to it, in how it articulates a dilemma that existed for much too long a time: the race problem. No other book recounted that experience both in terms of its effect on personal lives, and in a larger sense, on its place in Europe in the nineteenth century. Even today in the Academy, we are persuaded that Du Bois pretty well had the right take on it—on how the sense of color distinction, while it had always obtained, gained new reinforcement as imperialism became the defining factor of planetary life in the late nineteenth century, when Europe intruded into Africa and Asia. Du Bois was marvelous at contextualizing how color had become the anchor and the justification for the dominion of one group of people of one color over other groups of people of different colors. As a tool of analysis to understand not only one's personal dilemma and one's group dilemma, but also a global dilemma, *The Souls of Black Folk* was, and has continued to be, a template of group understanding and group defense. And what is so interesting is that Du Bois is at the center of everything; you either walk away from the book saying, This is an egomaniacal presence that disturbs, bothers, offends me—and I think many people feel that—or you say, This is truly a stellar mind and sensibility at work.

DO: Exactly. And his singular intellect is one of the many aspects of his character that you dramatize so skillfully in your biography. I'm hard pressed to think of another public intellectual in the past century who has come close to matching his influence in so many different spheres.

DLL: I think I would fully agree, except perhaps for Henry Adams. I've always thought of the two of them together. They're very different in their politics, to be sure, but both presumed to judge their time in a way that few writers do. Both are censorious, both are superior, both are aristocratic in their take on their times; they have a synoptic arrogance or synoptic wisdom, if you will, which you don't see so often.

But when I began wrestling with Du Bois's life there were times when I thought that maybe we were just on the edge of something clinical: For a man of twenty-five or thirty to think that through his life, the life of his times was to be apprehended, was maybe a little delusional. But then at the end of the day, you have to say that it *is* through his life that you can understand a great swath of history. Whether or not you sign off on his many, many positions and advocacies, his interaction with his times was in fact major, and therefore has to be taken with great seriousness.

DO: Was it his unique place in history that drew you to take on this fifteen-year-long project, or was it the fact that relatively few of your readers would be likely to appreciate already the magnitude of his contributions?

DLL: Both, I suppose. I thought it would be a terrific biography because somehow this important life hadn't been written up, and the documents—some 115,000 items—were just about to become available. I quite candidly acknowledge that it was the chase that motivated me: I wanted to get to the head of the queue for an opportunity that comes once in a lifetime, and I had the good fortune to be there at the right moment.

And then I thought, okay, this is a big life, I'll write about it in four hundred pages, and it will take four or five years, maybe a little longer. I suppose it was rather like walking onto the campus of Columbia and into Jacques Barzun's office and saying I want admission and a stipend—had I known the task ahead of me, I would certainly have been daunted. It was only two or three years later, as I finished most of the research, that I saw this was a titanic life, and that there were so many aspects of it that I hadn't thought I'd have to deal with. I hadn't expected to go to the Soviet Union and really get to know the Russians who had been in Du Bois's life, or to return to Africa to recapture that memory trace there, or to find members of the Communist Party of the United States who were involved in Du Bois's life. It became quite an enterprise. My wife could probably speak to that with even more...

DO: Feeling?

DLL: Yes. I learned as I went along also what a multitiered personality he was. For example, I had thought that because Du Bois was an historian that I would be able to work with what he documented, but I soon found that Du Bois was seldom to be believed; in fact, the more precise he was in his accounts, the less likely I was to find verisimilitude. And then the question was, Do I think less of him for this careful mendacity? But no, I did not, because from his point of view that mendacity was always in the service of a higher point; he considered it quite appropriate to shape the facts to an ideal. Of course, once I was alert to this, it was fun to do the kind of detective work that would reveal what I thought *really* had happened.

DO: You've said that "psychologizing" is "a thing that historians do at their peril," yet it's a challenge you take on fairly often in your first volume of Du Bois's life. Did the fact that he did everything for history, so to speak, make that challenge less risky or more risky?

DLL: I think both. For example, I found the way in which Du Bois told the story of coming of sexual age rather puzzling; it didn't jibe with my own puberty and post-pubescence, or that of my friends.

So dressed like Du Bois, I put myself on a couch with a psychiatrist and talked about "my" upbringing in Great Barrington and "my" mother. And out of that came a "Eureka" moment. Well, there's none of that in Volume One but when I told a reporter that I'd used this device and it came out in the newspaper, people said, Has Lewis taken leave of his historical training? Has he lost his mind? It was certainly an eccentric and anomalous way of getting at what I was trying to do, but I'm not ashamed of trying to find the kind of sensitivity that presses the documentary envelope. The biographer must try cautiously to put him- or herself into the moment when a decision is being made or an act is being performed, in order to give it its greatest explanatory resonance. And if that means putting yourself into the mind of your subject, I think you had better risk it; you at least had better write it out and see how it flows.

DO: You've described the first volume of your biography as the one in which you "wound up" Du Bois and Volume Two as your "Duracell battery volume," because he keeps going and going and going. Was this your narrative strategy from the outset, or did it develop out of necessity over time? How, in any case, did you keep *yourself* going over time?

DLL: Du Bois made the decision about two volumes, in that as I wrote what had been intended as a single volume, I saw that it would be an elephantine monograph. The more I thought about that problem, the more logical it became to split this virtually hundred-year-long life into equal parts. Indeed, the history of the times beckoned me to do that, as the divide would come at the end of World War I. So I breathed a sigh of relief, and embarked on the next chapter.

But then I had another thought: That while Volume One would focus on the "good" Du Bois, the Du Bois who wrote *The Souls of Black Folk* and edited *The Crisis* magazine and cofounded the NAACP, Volume Two would be about Du Bois the communist, Du Bois the expatriate, Du Bois the great contrarian. As it happened, the first volume appeared in 1993, only two years after the collapse of the Soviet Union. I hoped that the new Russia would emerge as democratic, and that the economic and cultural relations between the United States and the new Russia would grow; and I wagered that the longer it took to present the second volume, the greater the chance of Du Bois's apostasy being judged with a frame of reference less beleaguered by ideology. So that was another strategy that I hadn't thought about initially, but one that became a factor once I decided to write the second volume.

How to keep going, once I had determined to write the second volume, was another matter. For one thing, my wife kept me going, and I had a wonderful relationship with my editor. And then there was Du Bois himself: never a dull moment with him. Even my wife would concede that he was never dull, though she found his treatment of the people in his intimate life intolerable. But consider the alternative: I could have been writing about a man who was quite uninteresting. That's the worst dilemma a biographer can confront, and with Du Bois that was not ever a consideration. It seems to me that it is not the challenge of the biographer to redeem his or her person, but to let the life speak for itself. Yet the issues that some lives raise, say, about political or economic justice, are issues that many biographers cannot walk away from—and I found myself one of those. So in my personal life, if not in the written biography, I must credit Du Bois with forcing me to be more impatient with the wastage and failures of American political life than I had been before.

DO: And in fact that's the emotion you inspire in your readers.

DLL: I'm so pleased you say that because if I had one hope for this biography, it was that the reader would become aware of the gap between the ideal and the real, and the importance of feeling rage about not doing our best to make life better for as many people as we can.

DO: And you achieve that goal in much the same way as Lytton Strachey in his *Eminent Victorians,* another one of your favorite books. In his introduction he quotes a French master whose credo was, roughly translated, "I impose nothing, I propose nothing; I expose." Does that capture your own approach as well?

DLL: Yes, I think that's an accurate description of my motive and of my understanding of my responsibility. You know, there were two great biographers who invented the modern biographical form: Strachey and Froude, whose biography of Carlyle was the first big biography to look at the personal life and the affective life of his subject. Indeed, he exposed some of Carlyle's sexual peccadilloes and that, of course, was considered an utter no-no in Victorian England. Now that I think of it, Carlyle himself was a big factor in Du Bois's interest in writing and history, and Carlyle's history of the French Revolution has always been in the back of my mind.

I reread *Eminent Victorians* recently, and it stands up rather well. The book does what institutional history is supposed to do—it gives us the structure of the times and illuminates how those forces were ordered and set in motion. I just want to read to you an example of Strachey summing up, in a few deft sentences, one of the most important institutions of his day, in his profile of Cardinal Manning: "For many generations the Church of England had slept the sleep of the...comfortable. The sullen murmurings of dissent, the loud battle cry of Revolution, had hardly disturbed her slumbers. Portly divines subscribed with a sigh or a smile to the Thirty-Nine Articles, sank quietly into easy livings, rode gaily to hounds of a morning as a gentleman should, and, as gentlemen should, carried their two bottles of an evening. To be in the Church was in fact simply to pursue one of those professions which Nature and Society had decided were proper to gentlemen and gentlemen alone."

It's that kind of writing that I commend to myself and to anyone trying to write biography; the time and the place are recapitulated with economy and vividness.

DO: Some of the most profoundly radical notions that Du Bois advanced in his books and speeches—civil rights, cultural pluralism, pan-Africanism, African-American Studies—are accepted without question today, while other favorite themes, like double-consciousness and invisibility, are addressed routinely in both fiction and nonfiction. Yet some have said that as a writer, he was more interested in propaganda than in art or in scholarship. Is that a fair assessment?

DLL: No, it's not. Du Bois was able to do such a wide variety of things that one has to be very clear, it seems to me, about which thing Du Bois was doing when one is talking about him. In *The Crisis*, for example, he did a fair amount of what I believe was called, and perhaps is still called, contributionism—that is, he wrote about the first African-American to go to the North Pole, the first African-American to get a Phi Beta Kappa key, etc., because he wanted to increase pride. But he was very clear as a practicing historian about where propaganda must stop. His *Black Reconstruction in America* is not only his greatest work, but one of the most important works in American history. There you see him writing with ideas that do not desert the database he's using, and I think that is also true of his lesser known works, which were written in the late forties. Indeed, his take on the Reconstruction era finally came on-line in the sixties and seventies, and is reflected marvelously in Eric Foner's history of that tragic era.

But having said that, I think it's also fair to underscore the propaganda and to be worried by it. I have to put my cards on the table and say that his defense of Stalin and of Soviet tyranny was inexcusable. If Du Bois had been simply a politician, you'd say, More's the pity. But you must be much more severe with Du Bois because he wasn't a politician, or just a politician; he was so many other things, all of them flavored with principles and ideals. So when he turned his back and averted his eye to the gulag, that was really poor. As a biographer you explain it, but that doesn't mean you justify it.

DO: Du Bois's insistent question, "Would America have been America without her Negro people?" dates from 1903, yet it seems that Americans are still struggling to understand how we have become who we are. To what extent do the same received notions about our history and culture that so enraged Du Bois still prevail among students today?

DLL: On the graduate level the Du Boisian optic is, I think, fairly common as a means of analyzing the past; the undergraduates lag behind, I'm afraid. Nonetheless, it is my experience that while young people are inclusive in a way that Du Bois would applaud, they don't quite know how they got there; there's no memory trace of the things that Du Bois had to fight. For most students racism evokes very little, in real terms, and that is a good thing. And affirmative action, despite the fact that the courts keep revisiting it, is part of the way in which Americans live their institutional lives. So, much of what Du Bois inveighed against, and much of what he wished to see happen, is occurring.

But as George Santayana, one of his teachers at Harvard, famously said, Those who forget history are doomed to repeat it. And that is my concern, because a defining characteristic of American culture is amnesia on the one hand, and an unqualified belief in linear progress on the other. We don't look back—we look forward—and that results in all sorts of surprises when we discover that other people look upon us very differently from the way we see ourselves. We're moving into a different kind of racial dynamic in the United States and we're not thinking a great deal about what that will mean. For Du Bois, and for as long as the Republic has existed, that dynamic has been a kind of dyad of white Americans versus black Americans. But the twenty-first century is a century in which we will be dealing with white, black, brown, and yellow Americans. Indeed, demographic projections suggest that Hispanic Americans will become the largest minority, and that Euro-Americans will become a slight minority. Some would say, Well, that's wonderful. But even so, there will be problems with knowing what we are and what we want to be in terms of language, in terms of religion, in terms of culture, in terms of politics. One only need look to Canada to see how problematic two cultures, French and Anglo, can be. Now, I'm not for one moment suggesting that these are not healthy prospects and possibilities; but this new ethnic pluralism does carry with it challenges, and looking at the past will help us, to some extent, understand how to deal with the oncoming configuration.

DO: Lytton Strachey also writes in the introduction to *Eminent Victorians* that "ignorance is the first requisite of the historian." What is it that *you* want to learn more about? And what should historians be doing to help Americans cope with their amnesia about the past and blind faith in the future?

DLL: My new challenge is to write a book about Islam with the working title, *The Islamic Invention of Europe in the Eighth Century.* It is a challenge I took on before 9/11—I say this because I'm not simply joining the great rush to acquire Islamic expertise—since I had felt for some time undeniable signals that we were in store for some homeland attacks. The point of this meditation is to look at about sixty-five years in the eighth century when Arab, Berber, and other tribesmen invaded Spain, conquered it in very short order, and then streamed over the Pyrenees into what has become France. This blitzkrieg led eventually to one of the great conceptualizing documents of European history, "Le Chanson du Roland," in which the French defined themselves as a nation, as a race, and as a religion, in opposition to Islam. I want to explore these seeds of nationalism, intolerance, and feudalism, because it seems to me that the eighth century defined the way in which Christians, Jews, Muslims, and others now look at one another.

With this book I am moving from a pretty firm knowledge base with Du Bois to one that may appear to others to be quite a conceit, or certainly a big risk; but I'm enjoying it and taking my learning curve very seriously. My own personal take is that the role of the historian is to provide a faithful recapitulation of the past in a way that is vivid, vital, and valid. And since I think biography and history are one and the same, and since Americans, we are told, cannot get enough biography, historians have a wonderful opportunity to keep a traction on the popular imagination and the popular comprehension. We really must take advantage of that opportunity.

BOOKS BY DAVID LEVERING LEWIS

Prisoners of Honor: The Dreyfus Affair
District of Columbia: A Bicentennial History
King: A Critical Biography
When Harlem Was in Vogue: The Politics of the Arts in the Twenties and Thirties
Harlem Renaissance: Art of Black America (co-author)
The Race to Fashoda: European Colonialism and African Resistance in the Scramble for Africa
W.E.B. Du Bois: Biography of a Race, 1868–1919
The Portable Harlem Renaissance Reader (editor)
W.E.B. Du Bois: A Reader (editor)
W.E.B. Du Bois: The Fight for Equality and the American Century, 1919–1963

Readers who want to learn more about David Levering Lewis are urged to read some of the books that have made a deep impression on the author:

The Souls of Black Folk, W.E.B. Du Bois
Eminent Victorians, Lytton Strachey
Rousseau and Revolution, Will and Ariel Durant
The Development of Modern France, Denis Brogan
The Civilization of the Renaissance in Italy, Jacob Burckhardt
Social Darwinism in America, Richard Hofstadter
Black Jacobins, C.L.R. James
Marcel Proust, George Painter
The Rise and Fall of the Third Reich, William Shirer
The Waning of the Middle Ages, Johan Huizinga

BARRY LOPEZ

*National Book Award Winner Barry Lopez was born in Port Chester,
New York, in 1945, and was raised in Southern California and New
York City. A graduate of the University of Notre Dame, he moved to
Oregon in 1968, matriculating at the University of Oregon before em-
barking on a career as a full-time writer. In his nonfiction, he writes
most often about the relationship between the physical landscape and
human culture, as in* Arctic Dreams, *which was honored with the
1986 National Book Award for Nonfiction, the Christopher Medal, the
Pacific Northwest Booksellers Award, and the Frances Fuller Victor
Award for Nonfiction. Among his many other highly regarded works*

are the multiple award–winning Of Wolves and Men, Field
Notes, Winter Count, *and* Crow and Weasel, *which won a Parents' Choice Foundation Award in 1990 and inspired a stage production of the same name at the Children's Theatre in Minneapolis. His
work appears in dozens of anthologies and has been widely translated,
and his essays and short stories appear regularly in magazines and
journals including* Orion, The Paris Review, The Georgia Review, DoubleTake, *and* Outside. *A longtime contributing editor to*
Harper's *and the* North American Review, *he counts among his
many honors an Award in Literature from the American Academy of
Arts and Letters, a Lannan Foundation Award and Residency Fellowship, Pushcart Prizes in both fiction and nonfiction, the Antarctic Service Medal from the United States Congress, and honorary LHDs
from the University of Portland and Texas Tech University. A fre-
quent collaborator with artists in other media, he travels extensively
around the world, with recent trips to Cuba, Belize, South Georgia, and
Greenland. He lives on the McKenzie River in Oregon.*

DIANE OSEN: I'm always struck by how often and how carefully
you write about the varying qualities of light, not just in *Arctic
Dreams,* but in many of your other books, as well. What was the light
like in California when you were a boy? And how did the landscape
there shape your imagination?

BARRY LOPEZ: It was a saving light. My childhood was a difficult
one and my emotional sense of those years is that the light was a
kind of refuge for me, something on the order of a living thing, like
animals or trees. It was always dependable as a companion. If I felt
depressed or frightened I sometimes would just go outside and
stand in sunlight.

I had a very strong emotional attachment to elements of the
landscape around me. The area of the San Fernando Valley where
I lived wasn't spectacular; it was open space with alfalfa fields and a
big sky and distant mountains. So it makes some sense to me that

later in life I'm drawn to open landscapes like deserts or the polar regions—although ironically, I've lived in an old growth forest for the past thirty years.

I think the landscapes that stimulate you when you're a child are the ones you continue to imagine as dramatic settings, as you grow older. Probably what happens is that all the abstract ideas that we grow up with—love and truth and beauty—have to be dramatized for us in order for us to really understand them. They have to become real to our eyes in terms of human gesture. And for me, human gesture takes place in a specific environment—on a city sidewalk, or across a table, or in an open field, or standing on the beach watching waves crash. So when I think in the abstract about truth or beauty, I always imagine them becoming apparent through a gesture occurring in a place, and often for me that place is a more open landscape.

DO: You've written about how your life changed overnight when you moved into a New York City penthouse apartment at the age of eleven, and started attending a Jesuit prep school. To what degree did your experiences as a student spark your interest in two other notable—and possibly even related—features of your work: your love of language and your interest in different kinds of devotion?

BL: I don't think there's any doubt that when you go through the kind of prep school education I had—you're exposed to so much language and so much literature, it's inevitable that you develop a working vocabulary probably larger than most people's. But I wouldn't say that I fell in love more with words in prep school, or that I had clearer ideas about being a writer.

What's probably truer is that the transition from California provided me with an intellectual stimulus I would not have gotten there. In New York, I was emotionally stimulated by ideas and history and art in just as powerful a way as I had been emotionally stimulated by the landscape of California. By the time I graduated and got to Notre Dame, I had developed a love of language I was conscious of, which had grown up out of reading. I was tremendously influenced, for example, by the work of Gerard Manley Hopkins. In some of his poems there's an obvious focus on nature, but what Hopkins was really writing about was the relationship between humanity and the divine.

At Notre Dame my sense of beauty and the preciousness of human life—what you may be calling devotion—matured, too, not so much as an issue of religion, but as my attempt to try to locate a life that's divinely oriented in the world. Until I was twenty or twenty-one I mostly understood that in the context of Roman Catholic religion. But, unlike many of my friends, I never had a violent, angry break with the Church. I just walked quietly to the back of the chapel and didn't return, because while it is a beautiful liturgy, which in its best moments represents an extraordinary involvement with the holy, it is also exclusionary and I didn't, after a while, really like that.

Too much of Christian religion is rooted in the idea that the world is awful, and that what we all want is to escape it and get to another place which we call heaven.

But there is also a tradition in the Church that heaven is here— it's within us and it's present to our senses. I felt this as a child, standing in the light, or watching the wind flare the leaves of Lombardy poplars, or hearing the wind drive through the branches of eucalyptus trees. I had this wordless sense that I was in the presence of the divine. But as I grew older I never heard these things mentioned in the Church of which I was a part.

It wasn't until I began traveling with Native American people and with Eskimos that I realized many other peoples and cultures had lived for millennia with this same awareness that I had experienced as a child. The fact that you could sense the divine in the real world around you was no mystery at all to them; it was part of everyday life.

DO: That impulse to locate the divine in the everyday also informs the work of two of your favorite writers, John Steinbeck and Herman Melville. How has their work shaped your own?

BL: Often when talking about such influences, we're looking for dramatic turning points. We assume those authors the writer reads most avidly early on inform the work that comes afterward. If a writer is discovered to have read these three or four books when he was seven years old, if he recalls that fact thirty years later, it is assumed those books fixed a trajectory for his or her life. I think that's rarely the case. Rather, it's that both early on and all the way through your life as a writer, certain books change in a larger or smaller scale the way you approach your work—whatever it is. Steinbeck's work and Melville's work gave me a way to imagine my own life, even before I knew I wanted to be a writer. If you do become a working writer, and if your creative life continues to develop, there are going to be points throughout when you are reading a book that will alter the direction of your work. We think of "influence" as a carryover of technique or subject matter or politics, but I think it's really the shape of the imagination you respond to that carries over into your work as a writer, say as determination for a similar clarity or vividness in your own material.

I remember reading everything by Steinbeck through *Travels with Charley* before I was a freshman in college, and thinking, Gosh, I'm not alone. Here's a guy who's a great writer and he thinks about things in the same way I think about them. I was stimulated by his work because a lot of the novels, of course, are set in California, and he was oriented toward agricultural communities; he could evoke something mysterious in the land, and I felt that I knew what that was even though I was only fifteen years old. And I felt he was writing about concerns that were very much like mine in a way that I could understand.

Moby-Dick was influential because it made it possible for me to grasp a longing that I did not understand for years—which was a longing to tell a story. At least in that novel, Melville imagined a world that was very much like the world I wanted to live in—a combination of physical work and mental and emotional awareness. And in some odd way, the model for what I wanted to do as a writer was his narrator, Ishmael. He is a participant in the drama, and he's clearly interested in conveying what he knows to the reader; I always think of him as the reader's companion. He had a tone of voice that I liked, and I wanted to find a tone of voice that the reader would like, and to be useful to the reader in the same way that I thought Ishmael was useful.

Another huge part of this was that I wanted to deal with the real stuff—and for me, that was the relationship between the physical world, the world that we inhabit, and the divine world, or the oc-cluded, mysterious world. All of the apparatus for whaling, the boats and the lines and the harpoons and the oars and the sails, were things that were fascinating to me, as travel itself was fascinating.

An immersion in books as a child gives you a sense of the vast landscape of the language—and that's another element of *Moby-Dick* that appealed to me. When you look through all of those quotes at the beginning of the book, you may find some of the lan-guage arcane, but you don't resent having to look it up because there's a sense that you're onto something extraordinary. James Joyce, for example, did not write in a way that made him easily ac-cessible to a great many people, but part of our cultural admiration for his work comes from his ability to say exquisitely exactly what he meant to say. You admire a voice that's like no one else's voice speaking clearly about the things everyone wishes to know: What does it mean to be in love? What does it mean to feel grief? What does it mean to know ecstasy? When those things are confirmed for us in literature, the sense of loneliness that our culture exacerbates is assuaged.

DO: The importance of moving from isolation to connection—or what the narrator of *The Grapes of Wrath* describes as moving "from 'I' to 'we' "—is also one of the central concerns of your work. To what degree have your experiences in landscapes and communities different from your own shaped your interest in this notion?

BL: I believe very deeply that each of us is given a handful of ques-tions that are going to be our questions for a long time. They grow out of the emotional soil of our childhoods, and in the case of writ-ers, out of the books that we read. Depending on your skill and your inclination, you might spend your whole life addressing them. As you grow older and change, you might find yourself working in different genres, but often you're refining your responses to the same questions.

You know, I don't really write about landscapes, although some people say that. My subject, I think, is always the relationship between human culture and these places. I think anybody who sits down with the books I've written can step back from them and say, In these different forms, in these different ways, this man has been concerned with the same few questions for thirty-five years: What is the relationship of the individual to the divine? What is the relationship of the individual to the community?

I believe you can say that most English-language literature today is about community—what makes it coherent? What makes it fly apart? Can it be put back together? And I think this literature is generated by a fear that the disintegration of communities—families, neighborhoods, tribes—means an end to a fundamental part of human life. If I travel, say, in the Northern Territory in Australia and talk with aboriginal people there about the responsibilities and courtesies that obtain between an individual and the group, and then look at the way in which we in this country have indulged ourselves in extreme notions of individual privilege, and what that has done to our social fabric—that's something I want to write about.

Not a day goes by that I don't think about the fate of the culture of which I am a part, or about how writing a story can help. If, in essays or in short fiction, you can bring back the intensity of something forgotten or vaguely understood, by sharpening the image and making it succinct, then you're helping. A young person reading a story of yours could be inspired to attempt any number of things. An adult who has been abandoned by a lover or a child could read a story and find the reason that he or she wants to get up off the floor. All of those are good reasons to write. You're helping people do the things that are far more important than literature.

Every time I've been in an aboriginal village I've been reminded of that. My work means nothing in those contexts; nobody cares if you're a writer. They understand what a storyteller is, but what they want to know is whether you can fully engage with the real business of life—and the real business of life is taking care of each other. Just loving each other, and feeding each other, and building shelters together, and taking care of the children, and enjoying and intensifying the fruit of all of those bonds. There are so many distractions in modern life that I think we've lost entirely the sense of that. We are living lives of service to our distractions.

DO: Your career has been notable for many reasons, not the least of which is the choice you've made to address your "handful of questions" in both fiction and nonfiction. How difficult is it to move from one genre to another?

BL: I've forgotten who exactly this was, but a French artist recently said, If you find yourself in the middle of your life as a painter wanting to become a sculptor, you'd better change your name. What that means for a writer is that if your work in one genre becomes very well known, there's going to be terrific resistance to your writing in another genre. Reviewers are going to be trying to drag in all of this material from past work, instead of looking at the work at hand. And I think, too, that there is some resistance to the idea that the subject matter of anthropology or geography or natural history is suitable material for a literary writer. In the United States, for example, a writer like me is sometimes referred to as a nature writer, while readers in other parts of the world tend to regard the books as the work of someone interested in the same questions about community that interest most other writers. They aren't stymied by the metaphors.

About twenty-five years ago, I remember thinking that I wasn't going to write any longer about many of the things that were interesting to me because I felt my intent was so often misconstrued. But I couldn't develop any other sense of understanding about human fate without writing in a false voice, without violating what I saw as a writer's responsibility. Every writer has got to make peace with the fact that he or she is going to be misconstrued or labeled. You simply can't go out and correct that. The only response, I think, to criticism of your work, or to any misconstruing of you as a person, or to thoughts about where you may fit in the literary world, is to write another story.

DO: I know one of the things that fascinates you as a writer is what biologists call the ecotone, the borderland between one ecosystem and another. That borderland—biologically, geographically, culturally, even metaphorically—is in many ways the focus of *Arctic Dreams*. How did you come to write that book? And what inspired its unusual structure?

BL: Well, if the book has a beginning in time it was in June of 1978. I was with a friend of mine, a wolf biologist named Bob Stephenson, and we went far to the west in the Brooks Range in Alaska to camp for a while. While we were there I realized that I had been traveling back and forth to the Arctic with wolves as my only subject of inquiry [for *Of Wolves and Men*]. I'd missed a lot and I wanted to address that.

So for the next three or four years I traveled extensively in the Canadian and American Arctic and apprenticed myself to people who knew the place from different points of view. As was the case with *Of Wolves and Men,* I had no inclination to write anything definitive. What I wanted to write was something evocative—and that meant traveling with people who saw the world differently or whose education or whose language and experience were very different from mine.

In the beginning I had no outline for the book because I thought it would close the door on too much serendipitous encounter. But after two years the sheer mass of material I was dealing with had become so great that I decided to sketch in a platform on which the story was going to unfold. I started with the musk ox because, like us, it's a terrestrial mammal that lives in communities and it has a hierarchy of senses very much like ours. Then, with the polar bear, I moved off firm ground to a place somewhere between the ocean and the ice, with a mammal for whom smell and hearing are as important as sight. When I got to the narwhal, the rotation of the senses was complete—their sense of hearing is far more important than sight—and I was off firm land and into the fluid ocean. Then I introduced the idea of the unicorn, because I wanted to address, throughout the book, the crossover between what we know and what we imagine.

At that point I had my table set up with three large, exotic mammals on it, and I pushed the table a little bit to make them move with a chapter called "Migration." An important thing here for me was that once I started talking about that coming and going, the movements we call migration, I didn't stop and then start a new chapter about human migration. Human beings come into the drama as part of a biological world, rather than a cultural world. I wanted to underscore that biological relationship between people and a particular place. At that point, I could then open up the narrative to two distinguishing characteristics of the Arctic landscape: the variable nature of ice and the presence of light as a kind of animal. That middle section—"Migration" and "Ice and Light"— closes with a chapter called "A Country of the Mind," in which we clearly enter a landscape of the human imagination. The biological imagination of the opening chapters shifts to the authority of the literary imagination in the middle chapters, and the historical imagination closes the book.

The final, historical section was the one place I faced a technical problem. To that point I had been writing in the first person, but I was not present, obviously, in the early exploration of the Arctic by Western cultures. So I chose to do something that is unusual for me: I wrote about something dramatic that had occurred to me, not to someone else. We had had a difficult day once in the ice, when we were caught in the closing pack by a sudden storm and had a hard time getting out. So I recounted that, and began thinking out loud that what had happened to us was nothing compared to what the first Irish monks faced who sailed to the Arctic in carraughs. By doing that I freed up the historical voice that I use to tell the story of these explorations, but I think without losing an intimacy I'd tried to create with the reader in the first two-thirds of the book.

Once I had decided on the book's structure, my concerns were with finding a voice that conveyed enthusiasm for a place that, on first glance, seems not to be much at all; and with achieving a kind of intimacy with the reader that would lead him or her, at the end of the book, to say, Well, I don't think I would ever go to the Arctic myself, but I've loved this book. And I think, to a certain extent, that's what I'm after in all my nonfiction. I want to set up a series of relationships in the story, and a relationship between the story and the reader that will serve the reader even if he or she is not deeply interested in the subject. Because it's the *writing* in the story, and what that entails and what its effects are, that's important.

DO: Well, I have to say that I've certainly been thinking about how *I* might be able to go to the Arctic. But what I'm wondering is whether you have ever been struck by the similarity between the structure of *Moby-Dick* and *Arctic Dreams.* Both are epics that explore profound spiritual and moral questions, framed by the narrators' quest for self-knowledge; both alternate between exposition and narrative; and both are interwoven with a tremendous number of facts, data, testimonies, anecdotes, insights.

BL: That's remarkable. No, I'd never seen that. And it brings us back to your earlier question about reading. Maybe, as a young man of fifteen reading *Moby-Dick,* what I was thinking was, *This* is the way to tell a story. And when it came my turn to tell a story, that's what I did. A lot of my nonfiction work is a combination of narrative and exposition—and many pieces in *About This Life* and *Crossing Open Ground,* for example, are also framed by my travels. There is a tone of voice that I use that often suggests the epic. I'm always trying to explore questions of morality and behavior. So I think you're right; I don't resist at all the idea that there is a pattern in my work, or that it's like the one you've described.

DO: Speaking of patterns, you've written and spoken a great deal about the responsibility you believe that storytellers have to create patterns from which wisdom can emerge. What exactly do you mean by that?

BL: I think that in our culture writers sometimes are given the responsibility for being authorities when what they are really doing is reporting authoritative work. The authority lies with the story and with the antecedents of the story; the writer's authority is, I think, more limited. So if you read a book and you think it's very smart, it may well be that the writer is not the smart person, but that *you* are the smart person, because you have seen in the pattern the writer made some of the brilliance of life.

So, yes, I'm very comfortable with this idea that the writer is a person who recognizes patterns and who can re-create them on a page. It's the recognition of a pattern, a structure that can effectively or beautifully suspend something about what it means to be human, that compels you as a writer to tell that story. If you do it well, people of many different kinds will find something reaffirming or stimulating in the story. And if that's the case, then you've got to be at peace with what other people quite different from you make of what you've written. I believe a really good story is more profound than the writer herself or himself can ever explain.

In a culture like ours that exaggerates the importance of the individual, we've lost the sense that the impulse to tell a story is a social impulse. I don't deny at all that every writer is working out an individual artistic vision—but I believe that a large part of the urge to write comes from a desire to be part of society, to be involved in a substantial way in the fate of the people you love and are in a community with. Like anyone else, you hope people will say your life helped.

BOOKS BY BARRY LOPEZ
Desert Notes
Giving Birth to Thunder
Of Wolves and Men
River Notes

    Winter Count
    Arctic Dreams
    Crossing Open Ground
    Crow and Weasel
    The Rediscovery of North America
    Field Notes
    Lessons from the Wolverine
    About This Life
    Apologia
    Light Action in the Caribbean

Readers who want to learn more about Barry Lopez are encouraged to explore some the books that have shaped his writing life:

    Moby-Dick, Herman Melville
    The Grapes of Wrath, John Steinbeck
    Heart of Darkness, Joseph Conrad
    The Burning Plain, Juan Rulfo
    Arcadio, William Goyen
    The Man Who Killed the Deer, Frank Waters
    Portrait of an Artist with Twenty-Six Horses, William Eastlake
    Silent Spring, Rachel Carson
    The Plains Across, John Unruh
    One Hundred Years of Solitude, Gabriel García Márquez
    Far Tortuga, Peter Matthiessen
    Sound and Sense: An Introduction to Poetry, Laurence Perrine
    The poems of Gerard Manley Hopkins and Robinson Jeffers
    The novels of Thomas Hardy

DAVID MCCULLOUGH

A two-time winner of the National Book Award, the Pulitzer Prize, and the Francis Parkman Prize, and a recipient of the National Book Foundation Medal for Distinguished Contribution to American Letters, David McCullough was born on July 7, 1933, in Pittsburgh, where he was educated before entering Yale University. As a college graduation gift in 1955, he received from his aunt, Marty McCullough, a copy of Bruce Catton's A Stillness at Appomattox, *and "it*

was as if a window had been thrown open. It had the breath of life in a way I had not yet experienced. In retrospect, I know it changed my life."

Mr. McCullough published his first book, The Johnstown Flood, *some fifteen years later, having worked first as a writer and editor for publications including* Sports Illustrated *and* American Heritage. *His epic chronicle of the creation of the Panama Canal,* The Path Between the Seas, *earned him his first National Book Award in 1978, as well as the Francis Parkman Prize, the Samuel Eliot Morison Award, and the Cornelius Ryan Award. Five years later, he won his second National Book Award for* Mornings on Horseback, *which also received a* Los Angeles Times *Biography Award. His biography* Truman *won the 1993 Pulitzer Prize and the National Book Critics Circle Award, and was a Finalist for the National Book Award. His most recent book, the Pulitzer Prize–winning* John Adams, *was an immediate popular and critical triumph, hailed for its riveting portrait of America's brilliant and irascible second president.*

Long familiar to public television audiences across the country as the host of the highly acclaimed series Smithsonian World *and* The American Experience, *and as the narrator of documentaries including* The Civil War, *Mr. McCullough is one of the few private citizens ever asked to speak before a joint session of Congress. A past president of the Society of American Historians, and a member of the American Academy of Arts and Sciences, he is also the recipient of honors including the National Humanities Medal and the New York Public Library's Literary Lion Award. In the citation accompanying his honorary degree from Yale—one of thirty-one such degrees he has received to date—David McCullough was described as an historian who "paints with words," and was commended for giving his readers "pictures of the American people that live, breathe, and above all, confront the fundamental issues of courage, achievement and moral character." An avid traveler and landscape painter, he lives with his wife, Rosalee Barnes McCullough, in Massachusetts. They have five children and fifteen grandchildren.*

DIANE OSEN: What initially piqued your interest in history?

DAVID MCCULLOUGH: I suppose it was growing up in Pittsburgh in a family with stories of the old days there. My family had been part of the life in western Pennsylvania since the time of the Revolutionary War, and all that appealed to me very much. Also, I was a youngster during World War II, and I remember vividly the sense that what was happening elsewhere in the world was of greatest historic importance. Young men in the neighborhood who had gone off to the war came back and talked about it. All that was very exciting to me.

And we had plenty of books in the house: children's books, the Scribner's Classics—*Treasure Island, Last of the Mohicans, Mysterious Island*—with all those really stirring illustrations by N. C. Wyeth, which I loved to look at by the hour. I still do.

I loved the Carnegie Museum in Pittsburgh, with its displays of every imaginable kind. There was a model of the Parthenon with a light inside, and you could get up on a little step and look inside. And I loved movies about history, like *Sergeant York* and *Brigham Young*. Later I saw a stage production of *Inherit the Wind*. It was thrilling to see a real event of the past brought to the stage that way.

But certainly as important as anything were the teachers who made history come alive. I was lucky in my teachers. One of the lessons of history—one of the lessons of life—is that there is no such thing as a self-made man or woman. When I look back on my own life, I see more and more the extent to which I benefited from marvelous teachers and so many others who, whether they realized it or not, made being a kid a great time.

DO: Do you think of yourself first as an historian, or as a writer?

DM: I think of myself as a writer who has found in the past an opportunity for self-expression that for many reasons, some of which I'm probably not able to understand myself, appeals more than any other.

DO: When did you first think of becoming a writer?

DM: When I was in grade school. But it was not until college that I began to think seriously about it, though I never dared say so. There were others I knew at Yale who talked about being writers, but I never had the nerve or the presumption to say I was going to be a writer. I knew how far I had to go, how much I had to learn. Everyone needs an apprenticeship of some kind. Mine was at Time-Life for five years, and afterward as a writer and editor for the U.S. Information Agency, and after that for six years at *American Heritage* magazine.

Once I got going on my own work, I felt always that I was working in a tradition. I wanted to follow in the footsteps of writers I hugely admired who had not started out as historians or biographers, but who had found in history and biography the "place" where they could write: people like Bruce Catton, Barbara Tuchman, Paul Horgan, Walter Lord, Wallace Stegner—it would be a long list. The large past provides a way of saying things strongly felt. It's those stories that have such a powerful pull—that's foremost. I'm very much interested in the fundamental truth of what happened.

DO: I know that you first encountered Theodore Roosevelt when your brother portrayed him in a play when you were a child. What led you, as an adult, to focus on the story of his life in *Mornings on Horseback?*

DM: It's very easy to talk about why one character or another might make a particularly interesting subject. But in my experience, such questions have very little to do with the decision to proceed. It's more as if the subject reaches out and takes hold of you. You have to feel right about the essential idea of the book or it will be extremely difficult to sustain the work.

But of course there must be material to work with, and the Roosevelts were a family that wrote letters by the thousands and kept diaries that have survived. That kind of record offers the chance to get below the surface, which is really the writer's job.

DO: How did the book come to take its shape?

DM: In so many biographies the main character is seen to grow and change, while the people around him appear as more or less fixed entities. But that's not the way life is—everybody is always changing and growing, rising or declining—and so I felt it particularly important to see young Theodore in the context of his family, a composite of change all about him.

Mornings on Horseback is the story of the metamorphosis of a frightened, peculiar, sick little boy into a young man who will become the symbol of American vitality and purpose at the start of a new century. It's also a book about the influence of six people on one another. The family saves Theodore's life, both literally and figuratively, yet he can't ever become himself without breaking away from the family. His asthma is part of a handicapped, constrictive, sympathy-garnering childhood he must and will outgrow. It's only when he leaves home that he becomes Theodore Roosevelt.

This was a book in which I felt I had an opportunity to be perhaps more the writer and less the historian. The fact that the book doesn't begin with birth or end in death gives it a particular kind of freedom at each end. In many ways it's the most intimate of my books; I could expand the character because I wasn't obligated to do the whole life.

DO: You're working now on a book about another American president, John Adams, who is also the subject of a book that's had an influence on your recent writing life: Joseph Ellis's *Passionate Sage*. What was it about Adams as a character that reached out and lit your imagination?

DM: Joe Ellis is a superb writer, and *Passionate Sage* is, like his recent book on Thomas Jefferson [*American Sphinx*, Winner of the 1997 National Book Award], a joy to read. In reading *Passionate Sage*, I soon realized how much I didn't know about John Adams, and as so often happens, one book led to another and I found Adams to be an intensely interesting, intensely human being—unlike so many others from his time who, in imagination, seem more like figures from a costume pageant than actual flesh-and-blood men and women. I love Adams's language, for example; there is such a clear, sharp, unpretentious quality to it.

I had been thinking for years that I would someday write something about Thomas Jefferson, and it occurred to me that I might do Jefferson and Adams together, their intertwining lives. I got very excited about it. But I was concerned that Jefferson, with all that famous "aura," would be forever upstaging Adams. I mentioned this to my friend Richard Ketchum, whose wonderful book, *Saratoga*, was recently published. He said, "That's the least of your worries." And how right he was.

Novelists and playwrights talk about how characters begin to take hold and do unexpected things, and as a consequence the novel or play starts taking turns the author didn't expect. In a way that's what happened with this book. I was having a struggle trying to give Adams and Jefferson equal time, in effect, when it was Adams I wanted to write about. Once I saw that, once it became John Adams's story, I was on my way—happily!

DO: Ellis says, in *Passionate Sage,* that Adams was driven to sabotage his every achievement by a belief that popularity can never be compatible with virtue. Do you agree?

DM: That's a question I'm working with, but my way of dealing with or delineating the internal and external John Adams is through the telling of the story. I guess I've read nearly everything written about Adams in the last fifty years or more, but the great wealth of the material is in what Adams himself wrote—much of which hasn't been given the attention it deserves.

And there are sides to his life that I think need to be brought more to light. The importance of friendship to him, for example. Or the fact that he really did care about art and literature and science. His abiding love for his family. Here, after all, is the man who sired one of the greatest families in American history. And the importance of the fact that Adams had, as his life partner, Abigail Adams cannot be overstated. She was one of the most interesting, exceptional Americans ever—brilliant, learned, strong.

Whether Adams is a great man or a great president in the conventional, historian's way of seeing greatness may be arguable, I suppose. I don't think there's any question that he was one of the greatest Americans ever, and vastly, unjustly underrated. But what I love best is that he's such a great story. He does things, and things happen to him. He gets in trouble. He can be stubborn and grouchy and gloomy. He's brilliant. He's funny. And he tells you what he thinks—what he really thinks and feels—in no uncertain terms, and almost none of the others of his day did that.

DO: What are some of the challenges—and pleasures—of creating your own portrait of John Adams?

DM: I want the reader to feel—not just know—that other time and those other people. That's why it's so important to get inside the other time, inside the subject. I'm often asked if I'm working on a book, and I say, Yes I am. But what I really want to say is, No, I'm working *in* a book.

There's so very much with this project that I have to know about, the enormous number of people who figured in what happened. I'm venturing into the eighteenth century for the first time in my writing life—and what a good time I'm having reading those wonderful writers of the day, so many of whom we were required to read when we were too young. It's incredible how much they knew, how much they read, how much they wrote, how extraordinarily well educated they were. It's been one of the most stimulating experiences of my life.

Their letters are amazing. I try to read the actual letters, when possible. There's something about holding those pieces of paper in your hands. You have the feeling very nearly that you are the recipient of the letter—your hands are in the same place as the hands of Abigail Adams or Jefferson or Washington. And I don't care how experienced one gets working with historic documents—there is still something about it that sends a charge right up your spine.

DO: This is the third book you've written now that has focused on a president. How has your work affected your view of the presidency?

DM: We've had such different people serve in the office that it's very hard to make general observations about them. One lesson, certainly, is that exceptional presidents are truly the exception. They don't come along very often.

Generally speaking, those who've done best in the office have been those with a strong sense of history. And who respected the office itself, recognizing that they were only temporary occupants. Adams was the first president to occupy the White House— a new, very raw and unfinished White House. In a letter to Abigail he wrote, "Let none but honest and wise men rule here." Franklin Roosevelt had that line carved into the mantelpiece in the executive dining room, where for years now, the Healy painting of a rather pensive Lincoln hangs. It's very moving to stand there, and read those words of Adams's and see the portrait of Lincoln.

DO: You've told me that *Ben and Me*, by Robert Lawson, and Walter Lord's *A Night to Remember* are two of the books that changed your life as a boy and a young man. What was it about those narratives that so appealed to you then? And why do you admire them now?

DM: In the writing of history and biography, one has to call on imagination—in the sense of transporting oneself to that other time and those other people, all vanished, distant, and different. That takes research, and analysis of research, of course. But it also demands imagination.

What's so appealing about *Ben and Me* is Lawson's imagination. I adored the book as a boy. Reading it now, I see the author really knew his subject. There's a delightful incident in which George

Washington tells Ben Franklin they need money to fight the Revolutionary War, and that Franklin should go to another country to borrow some. Franklin can't decide—should he go to Spain? Germany? France? Franklin's small sidekick, Amos the mouse, who is the narrator, tells him, France, because the food is good there. And when finally Franklin goes to France, his and Amos's adventures are all set in a quite expert, knowing rendition of the real thing. Lawson understood quite accurately the details of Benjamin Franklin's life and the world of Franklin's travels and work, which gives the book great charm.

When *A Night to Remember* was first published in the 1950s, I thought it was about the best book I'd ever read: I was pulled into the story because of Walter Lord's exceptional narrative gift. And he does it all in less than two hundred pages! It is extraordinary. It's all been very skillfully pared down to the very essence. It's as if this is the only way the story could have been told.

When I set out to write *The Johnstown Flood,* my first book, I was greatly influenced by Walter Lord's example. I had not done extensive historical research before; I had been writing for *American Heritage,* as I've said, but a book is another matter. I had to figure as best I could how to do it on my own. And one thing I did was to take Walter Lord's book apart, so to speak, to study its architecture and try to see how he achieved such narrative power—how he managed to convey so much in relatively few words.

And isn't it marvelous to see *A Night to Remember,* forty-some years later, back up at the top of the bestseller list? Walter is an indefatigable researcher—he digs and digs and digs—but it's no easy matter to handle an event so tumultuous, so hair-raising, so tragic and so human, as the sinking of the *Titanic* and still to keep it within bounds, to make it clear and vivid.

DO: Despite all the hair-raising special effects in the film *Titanic,* I found Lord's account much more compelling—and I think that's because it features so many first-person accounts from people who were actually on board that night.

DM: Yes—there's no question about it. As Walter did for the book, I've tried, whenever possible, to reach a past event or time through living people.

There are good historians and biographers, particularly those with academic training, who disdain the personal interview on the grounds that memory doesn't serve—that people tend to distort things to their advantage, or simply don't recall things accurately. Well, that's often the way. But I also feel that what people may believe to have been the truth can be revealing in itself; and that the benefits to be gained from an interview, even with someone who may not remember everything precisely, are far greater than the risks involved, because there is so much one can learn of a kind that seldom turns up in conventional manuscript research. There's the idiom of the rememberer's recollections, the choice of words, the little things they recall about how someone sat at the table, or the sound of a voice, or the color of someone's eyes, which can't be found any other way.

DO: What responsibilities do you think a writer of history has to posterity?

DM: That's a big question. I guess I want very much for others to experience the enlargement of one's own life that comes with knowing about the lives and experiences and accomplishments and failings and voices of others who went before us. To understand that one need not be provincial in time any more than one would wish to be provincial in space.

I write what I do for the general reader, for everybody. Why labor over all the research and the thought and the reading and the writing to produce something that no one will want to read except possibly a handful of other historians? I hope other historians will read my work and enjoy my work, maybe admire my work. But I'm not writing for them; I'm writing for people like me. If I can convey how interesting the past really was, how full of life those people really were, what they were up against and how it turned out for them, then, my feeling is others will want to read what I've written.

And there's no need ever to trick things up, to sugar this or that, or use dramatic devices to make it interesting. You just try as best you can to make it as interesting as it actually was.

DO: To what do you attribute the enduring pull of the past on your imagination?

DM: A lot of people think of history as old dead stuff, and who can blame them? It's so often presented that way, like nasty medicine you have to take. I feel the story of our country is so strong, the richness and drama of it are so compelling, that I want to share the wealth. History is about life, about people—people, people, people—and I don't see why you, or I, or anyone, should limit those we know only to the brief time our biological clocks provide.

Every time I begin a book I think how much I'm going to learn. I hope my readers will learn a lot, too, and find as much enjoyment in that as I have. I'm seldom happier than when I'm creating something. When I have the research and my notes and my books stacked up about me, and I'm inside the work. One of the reasons why I enjoy the company of John Adams and Thomas Jefferson is that they made things. They wrote. They were builders.

It's a great thrill to have one's book published, to go into a bookstore and see your book there or see someone coming down the street holding a copy of something you've written. But the energy, the interest, the reward of the work comes from the work. And as much as I love writing history or biography, I might very well try something different sometime. Maybe a play. Maybe a novel. I don't know. That's part of the fun. You never know what bug might bite next.

BOOKS BY DAVID MCCULLOUGH
The Johnstown Flood
The Great Bridge
The Path Between the Seas
Mornings on Horseback
Brave Companions: Portraits in History

Truman
John Adams

Readers who wish to learn more about David McCullough are encouraged to seek out some of the books that have shaped his writing life:

A Stillness at Appomattox, Bruce Catton
Reveille in Washington, Margaret Leech
Angle of Repose, Wallace Stegner
Fifth Business, Robertson Davies
Wind, Sand, Stars, Antoine de Saint-Exupéry
My Antonia, Willa Cather
Passionate Sage, Joseph Ellis
A Night to Remember, Walter Lord
The journals of Eugène Delacroix
The books of Conrad Richter and Paul Horgan

ALICE McDERMOTT

National Book Award Winner Alice McDermott is the author of four widely acclaimed novels, including the recent Charming Billy, *which won the 1998 National Book Award and the Before Columbus Foundation Award, and* That Night, *a Finalist for the 1987 National Book Award,* The Los Angeles Times *Book Prize, the Pulitzer Prize, and a PEN/Faulkner Award for Fiction. Born in Brooklyn, New York, in 1953, she grew up in an Irish Catholic family on suburban Long Island and earned a B.A. from the State University of New York at Oswego and an M.A. from the University of New Hampshire.*

She published her first novel, A Bigamist's Daughter, *in 1982. Her third novel,* At Weddings and Wakes, *also a finalist for the Pulitzer Prize, was published in 1992, the same year that a film version of* That Night *was released by Warner Bros. She is currently the Richard A. Macksey Professor in the Writing Seminars at Johns Hopkins University in Baltimore, having served as a faculty member at the University of California at San Diego and at American University in Washington, D.C. She lives in Bethesda, Maryland, with her husband, a neuroscientist, and their three children.*

Hailed by The National Book Award's fiction judges for her sensuous, vivid prose, Alice McDermott "evokes the subtle yet fierce links between family and community" in a novel that explores the unbreakable bonds of memory that both distinguish and destroy the life of a charming Irish-American alcoholic. "Charming Billy *proves, once again, Alice McDermott's gift for revealing the essence of her characters' lives with patience and wisdom."*

DIANE OSEN: *Reader's Digest* can be found in the living rooms of any number of your characters. What was in the living room at the McDermott house when you were growing up?

ALICE MCDERMOTT: Well, *Reader's Digest* was there. And *Life*. And *The Saturday Evening Post,* from which my mother used to read aloud short stories that I was far too young to understand, but it was her way of getting to read them herself. And we had the typical New York newspapers. Both my parents were always reading something, but we didn't own a lot of books; we made weekly trips to the local library. Since my mother didn't drive, that was my father's job. He would sit in the newspaper section and we would have to bring him whatever we had pulled from the shelves, for his approval.

DO: So what kinds of books came home?

AM: I had two older brothers, so I followed in their footsteps and read all the boys' classics like the *Hardy Boys* series, *The Call of the*

Wild, and various war stories. I remember one specifically, because someone just a few years ago gave me a copy of it: *Fighting Father Duffy.* It was in our school library and my brothers took it out any number of times; and when I finally took it out, the librarian said I was the only girl to do so. It's a story about a priest who fights in the First World War and then takes care of these young, tough kids from poor neighborhoods in the city by beating them up. You know, setting them straight by whacking them around a bit and saying, Go to church. But it seemed to me that if my brothers were reading it, then it was worth reading. I was very disdainful of the things that girls were reading, like Nancy Drew; I wanted to read about a man's world. As I got a little older and women became more interesting to me, I began to choose my own books.

DO: When did you begin to think about doing some writing yourself?

AM: I was one of those kids who always wrote. I spent a whole summer writing a novel when I was about eleven, and I kept diaries that were mostly made up. I didn't have a real interesting life.

DO: I bet you did in your diaries.

AM: Exactly. And that's probably where and when fiction began to be appealing to me. I mean, I wrote all the time. My mother told me to. She told me very early, "If you get angry at someone or something's bothering you, don't say anything to anybody because when you're over it, the person you said it to won't forget, and you might get in trouble. But if you write it all down, then you'll feel better." And she used to do that. She used to sit at the kitchen table after dinner and write on paper napkins and then tear them up and throw them away. That was the advice I didn't follow—the "tear it up and throw it away" part. Growing up as a shy kid with two older brothers in a patriarchal, Irish Catholic family, the only time I ever got to complete a thought or to make a statement was if I wrote it down. For many children, I think, writing is a natural way of ordering the world. It wasn't till I got to college that I had the sense that writing was the only thing I wanted to do, not just a way to deal with life while I was doing something else.

DO: As you know, I'm sure, the story of how you came to publish your first novel, *A Bigamist's Daughter,* has taken on the dimensions of legend. What actually happened? And how did that enormous early success prepare you—or fail to prepare you—for the writing life of a novelist?

AM: I still believe I was extremely fortunate in the whole circumstance. I had finished graduate school and I wasn't really planning on writing a novel. When I told that to Mark Smith, a novelist I had studied with at the University of New Hampshire, he said, "Well, you *will* write a novel. And when you do, call me because I know an agent [Harriet Wasserman] who would be just the right person for you." Some months later I was living in New York, and when Mark was down on business I told him I *had* started a novel. Now, Mark was the person who had said to me in graduate school, "You know, *I'm* taking you seriously as a writer, so you've got to start taking *yourself* seriously." He said he was going to write to Harriet Wasserman and tell her that I'd be in touch. So I hand-delivered the manuscript because I felt so foolish even bringing it to the post office; I literally slipped it under Harriet's door and ran away. Then Harriet called and asked if we could meet, and suggested sending the book to Jonathan Galassi, who had just been made a senior editor at Houghton Mifflin. I had 100 pages, literally only 100 pages, not even page 101, by the time I went down to Jonathan's office. And I had a contract in another week.

DO: And that's why this story has become a legend.

AM: It had very little to do with me. I mean, it was simply good fortune that I had a friend and teacher like Mark to give me the encouragement I needed; and to have as an agent someone like Harriet, who respects writers and knows editors so well, and then to have Jonathan, at a very young age, take on the risk of publishing a first novel on the basis of 100 pages. I think this says there are people in publishing who really do care about books and want to nurture new talent. We don't hear that often enough about publishers.

As for preparing me for life as a novelist, it's hard to say. Certainly, having things fall into place in that way helped me to get that first novel finished—but I don't think it helped me to understand that I was a writer, or that writing was what I would be doing. I think I already understood that somewhere deep in my bones. As Harriet likes to say—wryly, which is her way—writing and publishing have very, very, very little to do with each other; almost nothing. For writers, it's a matter not so much of deciding you will write fiction with the hope that you will publish fiction, but rather writing fiction because there is nothing else you can do that will give you a satisfying sense of yourself or of life.

I often find myself beating the drum about this for my students, because early in your career it's very easy to lose sight of the fact that the work itself is the most essential thing. As frustrating and depressing and discouraging as a day spent writing can be, that day of work is also the best reward this career will give you. That's where your satisfaction has to come from—from creating those challenges for yourself, sentence by sentence, using whatever talent you have. You don't do it because you've got a contract with a publishing house. You do it because you have to, because that's what you're here for.

DO: I know one of the challenges you enjoy is focusing not so much on what happens in a story, but on who is telling the story and why. Emily Brontë was obviously drawn to that same challenge in *Wuthering Heights,* one of your favorite novels. How did reading the novel inspire that interest in both the storyteller and storytelling?

AM: The more I think about storytelling, the more valid it seems to me that the *impulse* to tell a story is as essential as the story itself. Just think about that early scene in the novel, with Heathcliff and his daughter-in-law and Earnshaw sitting around the fire, and that poor guy Lockwood trying to figure out who they all are. That's the delight that we get from stories: unraveling the complicated knots of family and relationships, figuring out how one little universe works. And how those knots get unraveled has to do with who is doing the unraveling, because who that storyteller is makes a difference in how the reader interprets who the other characters are. *Wuthering Heights* is probably one of the first books in which I got so caught up in that unraveling.

DO: Both of the primary storytellers in *Wuthering Heights* are very clear about accounting for the sources of their information, while in *Charming Billy* and *That Night*, the narrators simultaneously belong to and imagine the stories they tell. What inspired you to create these kinds of storytellers for these particular novels?

AM: With *That Night*, the first-person narrator was there in my original, vague intentions for the story. I had been working on another novel, but the characters were starting to have longer and longer conversations—these great chunks of storytelling and recollections—that were distracting me from what I thought I was supposed to be doing. Obviously I needed to write something about a collective memory, with a first-person narrator casting back over an event and over time, and putting things together.

Now, as soon as you have a collective memory you have various versions of it; and as soon as you have a collective memory over time you have conjecture, because over time what we think may have happened, or what we assume to have happened, becomes as much a part of our memory as those things that were clearly and absolutely observed. None of us, in relating stories, sticks to the facts. So the circling in the structure of the novel was very much a part of that convergence of retelling and imagining.

Having a first-person narrator recalling the past was not my intention when I started writing *Charming Billy*; that first-person female voice just popped up. I tried to write her out a number of times, because I was very tired of first-person novels—I think they are limiting sometimes—but then as I began to understand what the story was, I began to understand the narrator's role. The memory of Billy is in some way a collective memory, and in his milieu it is women who collect stories and hear everybody's anecdotes and make guesses and pass it on. So it seemed to me that it should fall to a female narrator to begin to put together and somehow figure out Billy's life. It also struck me that while you can find plenty of examples of first-person male narrators who are not trying to figure out their own lives, as soon as there is a first-person female narrator, she is gazing at her navel. So I was tempted by the idea of a female narrator who was more interested in other people's lives than in her own. A narrator to fully enter into Billy's story and reimagine it for the reader.

DO: Storytellers also figure prominently in *Absalom, Absalom!*, another one of your favorite novels. When did you discover that book, and what was your initial reaction to Faulkner's storytelling?

AM: I discovered *Absalom, Absalom!* in college, when I was in England for my junior year. Certainly, the initial appeal to me was the onrush of language in the novel, and just like *Wuthering Heights*, the story it tells is full of passion. But there's nothing more passionate in that book than the relentless demand that the story must be told, again and again. The sentences themselves contain that passion. The breathless desperation to get it told, to pass it on, to explain it to someone else—that's the thing that caught me up. That and the sense that the telling of the story itself is of great value.

DO: That's a quality found in your novels, as well.

AM: I'm not terribly interested in plots, and am always a little skeptical of stories that are too neat or too familiar. It's not surprising then that my interest most naturally goes to the "why" of the storytelling rather than the "how" or the "who" of the plot. That's the thing that *Absalom* reinforced for me—that the storyteller and the impulse to tell a story are as interesting as the plot.

DO: What else about Faulkner's approach to his work, or his beliefs about literature, have influenced your own writing life?

AM: His language—the permission he gives us to let language be lush but not wasteful, the passion for language contained in each sentence. And the idea that there are many ways to tell a story. You don't have to have a rising action and climax.

DO: Your own books, certainly, don't depend on that kind of structure, or even on a logical chronology.

AM: But in all honesty, I don't proceed with any literary theory in mind. All I have is a guess about what the story requires. There's something Eudora Welty said, about how when you're writing well you hear the sound of the next sentence before you know what the words are. In some ways there's that same sense in the structuring of a novel: before you even know exactly what the next step is, you have a full sense of what the next step needs to be. That's not to say that your instincts are always exactly right; finally it has to come down to what the work requires. So I would never say, "Well, I don't like chronological narratives," or "I will never write a chronological narrative." I would love to write a chronological narrative; I love reading them. But the stories I've told thus far have demanded something else of me.

DO: One of the other challenges you enjoy creating for yourself is taking stock characters and making them fresh and surprising. How did you first become interested in this? And what were some of the special challenges of reimagining the two stereotypes at the center of *Charming Billy* and *That Night*—Billy, the kindly Irish-American alcoholic, and Cheryl and Rick, the alienated teenagers in love?

AM: I think my initial interest in stereotypes had a lot to do with contrariness. I have this reluctance to write about a character who sounds really interesting, and a reluctance to write a novel about anything that I can summarize in three or four lines. But to stay with a character over the course of time it takes to write a novel requires more than just contrariness. The ability to individualize a character, to know another life as intimately as we know ourselves, is one of the marvelous gifts that fiction gives us.

Billy was a big part of my initial impulse for the book, because there seems to be just such a stock character in so many extended Irish-American families. But the challenge that appealed to me was not taking someone who appears to be a stereotype and revealing him to be much more complex, or ironically, quite the opposite, of what he seems. To me, the challenge was to take a character who is deep in his soul all the things you would assume him to be, and still to make him an individual, and to make clear the very particular and important role he plays for the other people in his life.

As for Cheryl, the fact that she is stereotypical in her description and circumstances gave me the courage to make her more complex in her personality. The fact that she is outwardly stereotypical frees her to be something else, to have a quasi-spiritual inner life that is completely separate from the way she appears. I liked the odd, unexpected strength of someone who conforms in that way to ensure her privacy. And it makes her that much more appealing to Rick, the single person that spiritual life is revealed to. But Rick is more like Billy. The stereotype goes deeper; he's more what he appears to be. And yet he recognizes that thing in Cheryl that's unique and scary and fascinating, and it makes her that much more appealing to him.

DO: Many readers assume that your novels are autobiographical, so let me ask you this on their behalf: To what degree is your fiction shaped by your own experiences?

AM: You know, I had a great experience in a bookstore in La Jolla, California, when I was doing a reading to promote *At Weddings and Wakes*. On one side of the bookstore, a guy raised his hand and said, "Is this your family?" And from the other side of the bookstore a woman yelled out, "No, it's mine!" And I have to confess that I like fooling people into thinking I write about my family, but in fact I don't write about my own immediate experiences. Certainly, I write about what I guess you could say I know, as far as setting goes. And certainly I write out of my experience of hearing how people talk to one another, and seeing how people deal with each other. So I don't write characters who are totally detached from myself and from my own experience.

Actually, my students and I talked about this just this past year, and we came to the conclusion that really what writers want is the *aura* of autobiography. You want the reader to have a sense that you know these characters so well you must know them in your own life. I think a lot of us who write fiction are probably reformed liars, because the impulse to lie is awfully close to the impulse to tell stories. And any good liar knows that you always mix up something that really happened into the story of something that didn't happen because it gives your lie authenticity. I couldn't write anything that actually happened because the impulse to change it would be too severe. That's why I write fiction, because fiction is a way of ordering the world, and in making the world orderly you have to change it, because it is not orderly on its own. Fiction is art, and the demands of art don't allow for anything to be taken whole cloth from real life. The color of a character's blouse and the wave of her hair and the shape of her cheek are not arbitrary decisions. They're part of the author's intentions for the entire work, so each detail must be chosen with those intentions in mind. If a book is any good, there can't be any irrelevant detail anywhere—and life is full of irrelevant details.

DO: They may not be inspired by your own relationships, but I think it's fair to say that your characters reflect your own interest in what it means to be part of a family. What is it that attracts you to that theme?

AM: Well, I suppose that writing about Irish Catholics in New York is writing about material at hand; I don't have to consult with anyone to find out what jokes they would tell each other at somebody's funeral. So in some ways, writing about family is the same. I know something about families. But I have no inherent interest in Irish Catholic families in New York as such. I think the great drama of most of our lives takes place in families, and my interests as a writer really come down to how we live, how we deal with one another, how we make sense of our brief lives. And one way to begin to write about that is to write about an Irish Catholic family in New York.

DO: As Dennis points out in *Charming Billy,* "It's hard to be a liar and a believer at the same time," and all of your novels, in one way or another, address the difficulties of finding and sustaining religious faith. How have your own attitudes toward faith come to shape your work?

AM: I think there comes a point in your writing life—and it comes again and again—when you're able to divest yourself of all other concerns about your career, your readers, your publisher, about paying the bills, and you understand that the work is the only thing that matters. It follows very quickly that since the work is the only thing that counts, you must write about the truest things you know. And time and time again what it comes down to for me is that faith—our need for it, our struggle with it—is the most important thing. But as I say, it's not something that you decide once, nor is it something that you're sure to achieve again and again. You never have the sense that, "Ah, I have now said the truest thing. And I'm going to go and say it again." It's more like, "I'm attempting to say the truest thing I know about us, about our existence, about life, and I'm attempting to do it in the best way I know through language. And of course I haven't done it yet."

Understanding the value of literature, and taking on a vocation of trying to add some small piece to its value, has helped me to understand my own faith. Recognizing the things that make literature a work of art—its essential truths—has made me a Catholic, or made me a Christian, in a way that being raised as a Catholic and a Christian was never able to do. That's just a personal outcome, but I think it says something about the value of art that when we're able to recognize its truth, it speaks to the things that make this short and often annoying life worthwhile.

This goes back to what we started out talking about, *Wuthering Heights* and *Absalom* and the impulse to tell the story. Because I'm interested in that impulse, I've come to regard it as something more than a kind of personality tic among humans. I'm loath to put it into language, because it sounds a little bit too touchy-feely even for me to bear, but the impulse to make art, to use language to offer our experiences to one another through fiction, and the almost breathless, passionate desire we have to tell and retell a story, says something to me about how we have been provided with the means of our own redemption. There is an answer to our cries into the darkness of "What is this all about, and why are we here?" Art is an answer. And literature is an answer. Not a blatant one, and certainly not a simple one, but an answer.

BOOKS BY ALICE MCDERMOTT
A Bigamist's Daughter
That Night
At Weddings and Wakes
Charming Billy
Child of My Heart

Readers who want to learn more about Alice McDermott are encouraged to seek out some of the books that have changed her writing life:
Absalom, Absalom!, William Faulkner
Wuthering Heights, Emily Brontë
To the Lighthouse, Virginia Woolf
Our Town, Thornton Wilder

CYNTHIA OZICK

A two-time Finalist for the National Book Award and winner of the 2000 National Book Critics Circle Award for Quarrel & Quandary, *Cynthia Ozick was born and raised in New York City. She graduated from New York University in 1949 and earned a master's degree from Ohio State University in 1950 before embarking on an apprenticeship that culminated with the publication of her novel* Trust *in 1966. Among the works that have followed are three award-winning collections of short stories—*The Pagan Rabbi and Other Stories, *a Finalist for the National Book Award;* Bloodshed and Three

Novellas; *and* Levitation: Five Fictions—*as well as the essay collections* Metaphor & Memory, Fame & Folly, Art & Ardor, *and* Quarrel & Quandary; *the novels* The Cannibal Galaxy, The Messiah of Stockholm, *and* The Puttermesser Papers, *a Finalist for the 1997 National Book Award; and a play,* The Shawl, *based on her novel of the same name.*

She is the recipient of honors including the Lannan Foundation Literary Award for Fiction in 2000, the American Academy of Arts and Letters Strauss Living Award, four O. Henry First Prizes, the Rea Award for the Short Story, as well as numerous honorary degrees.

Hailed by critics as a "writer's writer" equally adept in any genre, Cynthia Ozick is unparalleled in the range of her subjects, the comeliness of her sentences, and the passion of her tales. In The Puttermesser Papers, *written over three decades, she traces the history of Ruth Puttermesser, erstwhile attorney, mayor, and impersonator— a character so distinctive and unforgettable that she ranks with Huck Finn, Elmer Gantry, and Ralph Ellison's Invisible Man in our literary pantheon. The novel, said the judges of the 1997 National Book Award, "is what American fiction ought to aspire to be."*

DIANE OSEN: You've said that you felt you wanted to be a writer from the time you were first conscious of being alive. What, at that time, did being a writer mean to you? And how did that definition evolve?

CYNTHIA OZICK: I always wrote, and I always had writing as an ambition. One of my uncles was a poet, so I knew from my earliest years that one could grow up to be that. I remember composing a poem at the age of five, before I could read or write; my mother was my amanuensis. I retain only the opening two words: "O moon!" That's my first memory of writing, and gives me something in common, after all, with the later Henry James: dictation!

As I grew older, the images of bleak yet rapturous imposture— particularly in fairy tales—aroused an inescapable sensation of wanting to write. Princesses turned into mute swans, princes into beasts. Think of the eerie lure of the Pied Piper! I began to pursue that truly voluptuous sensation in middle childhood. I recall having written a story at the age of eleven, and afterward finding it an embarrassment; so I signed it, self-consciously, "By the Young Author, Age Nine." Another imposture. It might, I thought, have been adequate for a nine-year-old, but not for a serious writer of eleven. I wrote poems and stories and essays all the time, right through adolescence.

But at seventeen, as a freshman at New York University, I felt a certain turning in the cadence of my sentences; I suppose it was the beginning of a maturer style. One of my professors, who taught a course on the English poets, actually confirmed this. His name was Varney, and as a Greenwich Village poet himself, he had a certain authority and glamour. To my lasting delight, he wrote the word "professional" across one of my papers: a sublime moment. All the same, I believed it would be a long, long time before the word could realistically apply. Despite the force of my ambition and yearning, I felt insufficient and unready; in those days one was in a state of reverence for one's elders: teachers, professors, the distant powers who ran the publishing houses. And at the same time I believed that if I did not publish by the age of twenty-five, I would count as a failure. I did, in fact, count as that, and for many years—a thing that's left its mark. So many writers close to me in age had rocketed into the great world in their twenties: Styron at twenty-five, Mailer at twenty-five, Updike at twenty-four, and so on.

DO: I know that Henry James's *Washington Square* is a novel you're especially fond of. What is it about that book that struck you particularly?

CO: One day when I was seventeen years old, my brother brought home from the library an anthology of mystery stories that, oddly, included James's "The Beast in the Jungle." Reading it, I felt it to be the story of my own life—which was strange, since it's about an elderly gentleman who suddenly discovers that he has wasted his years. That's when Henry James first gripped me: He offered a premonition of the dangers of obtuseness, and of obsessive dedication.

Washington Square I came on much later, though it is in every way far more accessible than "The Beast in the Jungle," or the novels of James's later period, when his language became more densely convoluted. The story of Catherine Sloper is direct, moving, shocking. The theme of imposture runs all through: a harsh and relentless father impersonating a concerned and loving parent; a fortune hunter impersonating a sincere lover; a flibbertigibbet aunt impersonating a reliable confidante. At the end, Catherine, the victim of all of these, is impersonating the Catherine she used to be; the tragedy of her abandonment has made her into a different woman. When Morris comes to retrieve her at last, it is with the belief that she is the old Catherine he knew decades ago; and for a few moments she does indeed impersonate the old Catherine. But she has become a wounded, cold, vengeful, punishing, vindictive, self-preserving creature.

The idea of impersonation, I think, is central both to how writers think and imagine, and to what they write about. Not that all writers are drawn to impersonation as a theme; but all writers enact impersonation in the invention of character. One caveat: Writers who are impersonators in life cannot be honest writers of fiction. The falsehood will leach into the work.

DO: And that's because those writers have no authentic self, and hence lack authentic imagination?

CO: Exactly. The imagination that deals with fictive authenticity depends absolutely on personal authenticity, because fiction depends on clarity of seeing. If you are not lucid about yourself, you are not going to be lucid about anything.

DO: Another book that's strongly influenced your writing life— E. M. Forster's *The Longest Journey*—seems to me to confirm that connection between self-knowledge and the imagination. Rickie wants to be a writer of fiction, but one of the reasons he fails is that he's always trying to impersonate someone else—not unlike Ruth in *The Puttermesser Papers*.

CO: Whenever I think of *The Longest Journey*, what I remember most of all is the quiet yet perilous foreshadowings of the very first chapter, when Agnes is visiting the young undergraduates at Cambridge. She makes a little speech that is meant to be charming, but it contains a fatal imposture. Speaking on behalf of Rickie, and without consulting him, she says "we." Rickie's friend Ansell notices this right away, and condemns her ever after. Ansell is shocked again when Agnes, glibly and playfully, remarks that Rickie deserves to be horsewhipped. It is only a way of callous teasing, but it carries sinister seeds for the future. That "we" is saturated in arrogance and gall, in the usurpation of another's soul. If you look at Agnes's rather pale and pedestrian life as it evolves, it doesn't seem like a wicked life at all; but in arrogating Rickie's life to her own, in destroying his innerness, and in her want of any self-knowledge or imagination, Agnes surely embodies a genuine cruelty.

For a very long time I would read *The Longest Journey* at least twice a year. To borrow Forster's own phrase, it educates the heart. I was a college freshman when I first read this novel—it was a rich and inspired course assignment—and each time I returned to it, I uncovered more and more about human character, and especially the dangers of usurpation. Ruth Puttermesser is given to certain usurpations, though more as an act of folly than of wickedness. At one point she believes she can impersonate George Eliot, and attempts to seduce Rupert Rabeeno into joining her as a companion-impersonator. But Rupert is actually an impersonation of Puttermesser herself. I sometimes think of him as a kind of phantom projection of Puttermesser, a shadow of her own brain: Puttermesser, let us say, impersonating Puttermesser.

DO: Some of your readers may not realize that *The Puttermesser Papers* was composed over the course of several decades. What initially inspired you to create the character of Ruth, who is utterly unlike any other character I have ever encountered?

CO: I knew from the very start that this was going to be a novel, and that I would write it over a long period. It was a kind of experiment.

The original idea was to write one chapter per decade, though it didn't quite work out that way. But once I had this character, I thought I would just wait until some event or impression turned up that would stir her. When I became enchanted by the notion of the golem—in Jewish legend, a kind of Frankensteinian creation—it seemed to me that nothing would suit her more. And when I discovered in a biography of George Eliot that John Cross, her young husband, had jumped out of the window of their hotel room during their honeymoon, I instantly understood that this extraordinary leap belonged to Puttermesser's mind and world.

Where did Ruth Puttermesser come from? God only knows. She was just there one day, and I suppose the experiment succeeded in a sense, since I was able to bring her from her early years to her death, as I had planned from the start. You can see—it hovers over the very first chapter—that she was destined to have some dreadful New York crime befall her, though I had always surmised it would be something like a street mugging. I never dreamed that it would happen at home, in her own bedroom, while she was absorbed in reading Thomas Mann; but I always knew she would die a violent death.

DO: Did your ideas and emotions about Ruth change over the years as you told her story?

CO: No. She was always present for me, as a concrete and known character. I've always felt for her; I've always known her. She never changed.

And that, of course, is her great, deep flaw: her fixity, her inflexibility, her obsessiveness. She's got her back turned to the world. She is unable to experience experience, even as she's experiencing it. There is always the overlay of the imagination, usually the literary imagination, on top of real incident and ordinary life. She interrupts real life, even eschews it, in order to imagine a different order of living. She is a kind of monster, a possessed mind. There's comedy in such a creature; I think of her as a New York Don Quixote.

For example, when she first encounters the copyist Rupert Rabeeno in the museum, there's a momentary dissociation: She abandons the scene for a drink of water, and when she returns, the sight that so much lured her is altered; it's not the same. Something else is happening, and the genuinely interesting incident, a copyist meticulously reproducing on a canvas of modest size the enormous classical painting on the museum wall, is over. She breaks into and disrupts what most engages her. The germ of this scene came to me when I was visiting the Louvre some years ago, and saw the amazing reproductions of the copyists whose easels swarm in those galleries. And then, inevitably, I thought, Ah, this is for Puttermesser! But unlike Puttermesser, I never went away; I stood my ground and waited and watched, and watched and watched. Puttermesser intervenes in her own experience. She's always been like that, ever since I first knew her.

DO: You say you always knew Ruth's life would end. Did you always plan to end her story in a Paradise that's also hell?

CO: Well, when I came to the last chapter of the novel I thought it would be a fine thing to connect it to the beginning—and when I looked back to the first chapter, written three decades earlier, I was reminded with pleasure and surprise that I had already foretold her sojourn in Paradise, and even described what she would do there. What I did not know at the start was that Paradise, which I then believed was eternally paradisiacal, would turn out to have serious problems of its own.

And in the final chapter I made discoveries that reversed and contradicted the past. For instance, when I was writing the beginning, I thought that Puttermesser really had a sister in Calcutta, as well as a New England grandfather in a captain's hat. But now it occurred to me that those so-called biographical facts were not facts at all; they were fantasies and imaginings that Puttermesser, in her characteristic way, had substituted for real life. The mugging, as I've said, was predestined, though the location was not what I had anticipated. The second encounter with Paradise was partly predestined and partly an opportunity.

DO: You told an interviewer once that while you are "hostile to the whole mystical enterprise," you are nonetheless fascinated by the "mystical blur between the creator and the created." That blur is so important in *The Puttermesser Papers*—I'm thinking particularly of "Puttermesser Paired" and "Puttermesser and Xanthippe"—but it figures quite prominently in your other work, as well. Why has it come to have such resonance for you?

CO: My response to the mystical world is twofold. On the one hand, in the real world I reject it utterly; I am a rationalist. The mystic is dedicated to fusion, to blurring the difference between Creator and creature. The mystic believes that the Godhead can enter the human soul, that the human being can be filled with the Godhead. Quite aside from its hubris, I don't think we ought to live under such a delusion—that is, in the belief that one can summon God to do one's bidding, or that the creature can manipulate, much less contain or swallow, its own Creator.

But on the other hand, mystical notions are enormously exciting for fiction. There are few stories that can do without them. Storytelling is itself a mysterious blur of creator and creation. I think of the famous comment about Gershom Scholem's work on Kabbalah, the mystical current in Judaism (though far from Judaism's mainstream): Nonsense is nonsense, but the study of nonsense is scholarship. For me, mysticism is foolish self-deception, but the use of it in fiction is inspiration. Or put it this way: Mysticism is nonsense, but the enactment of mysticism in storytelling is rapture. Or is, to render a tautology, fiction.

DO: Critics have written a lot about your place in contemporary letters, particularly as a Jewish writer. In what literary tradition do you locate your sensibility?

CO: Isaac Bashevis Singer once said that every writer needs to have an address. Why else do we speak of Chekhov, Dostoyevsky, and Tolstoy as Russian writers, and of Jane Austen and Dickens and George Eliot as English writers, and of Jorge Luis Borges and

Gabriel García Márquez as South American writers, and so on? In this connection, and in nuance and perception (and with conscious respect for the obvious differences in stature and renown), I am a Jewish writer as John Updike is a Christian writer, or as V. S. Naipaul is a Hindu writer, or as Salman Rushdie is a Muslim writer. I have been enchanted by Jewish fable (the golem tale, for instance) or struck to the marrow by Jewish historical catastrophe (as in the little book called *The Shawl*). It is self-evident that any writer's subject matter will emerge from that writer's preoccupations, and it goes without saying that all writers are saturated, to one degree or another, in origins, in history. And for everyone alive in the century we have left behind, the cataclysm of murder and atrocity that we call the Holocaust is inescapable and indelible, and inevitably marks—stains—our moral nature; it is an event that excludes no one.

And yet no writer of stories should be expected to be a moral champion or a representative of "identity." That way lies tract and sermon and polemic. When a thesis or a framework—any kind of prescriptiveness or tendentiousness—is imposed on the writing of fiction, imagination flies out the door, and with it the freedom and volatility and irresponsibility that imagination both confers and demands. I have never set out to be anything other than a writer of stories. It disturbs me when, as sometimes happens, I am mistaken for a champion of identity in the currently fashionable multicultural sense, with its emphasis on ethnic collectivities. (The Greek origin of the word "ethnic," by the way, refers to anyone who is neither Jewish nor Christian. One of my dictionaries defines ethnic as "pagan.")

So if I had found myself consciously writing, as your question suggests, out of the literary tradition I have deepest access to (though via translations readers and writers can own the globe), I suppose I would have been something else: an academic in the Department of English, perhaps. "Tradition" invokes a kind of principled awareness; it carries with it a shade of teacherliness, of obligation. But as a writer I feel responsible only to the comely shape of a sentence, and to the unfettered imagination, which sometimes leads to wild places via wild routes. What could be more perilous than to mistake a writer for a communal leader, or for the sober avatar of a glorious heritage? No writer is trustworthy or steady enough for that. But above all, the aims of writers are the aims of fiction. Not of community service or communal expectation.

A generation ago, the British critic F. R. Leavis noted that George Eliot's *Daniel Deronda*, a novel written in passionate advocacy of the Zionist cause of Jewish restoration to the ancestral land, falls into two parts: one successful as literature, the other successful merely as didacticism. According to Leavis, only that portion of the narrative concerned with Gwendolen Harleth is novelistically alive. I think he is right. When I am looking for moral principle and virtuous dedication to historical justice, I am filled with admiration for the Zionist half of *Daniel Deronda*. But when I am looking for what stops the heart in the novel, I am solely with Gwendolen. And interestingly, the classical Hebrew writer (and Israeli Nobel laureate) S. Y. Agnon, who writes with extraordinary scholarly fantasy out of the marrow and soul of the ancestral land, is always novelistic and never didactic. He writes, in short, out of an address.

DO: What responsibilities, if any, do you think an imaginative writer has to his or her audience?

CO: The "if any" in the question implies the answer—or, anyhow, my answer. As I've already remarked, the writer's responsibility is not to the audience, but to the art. May I turn the question around, and ask what responsibilities readers have to a writer? Readers are either drawn to certain writers or they are not. Yet just as a reader may judge a book, a book can judge a reader. To dismiss Shakespeare, for instance, is self-condemnation. To choose to remain ignorant of history is autolobotomy. To run after trivia—exclusively after trivia—is a waste of life. Serious and genuine reading enables us to understand that ideas are emotions, and that emotions are ideas; and that is what we mean when we speak of the artist's imagination. If a writer can engender and illumine this understanding in a reader, that is something far better than "responsibility," with all its organized civic overtones. It is the enduring gift of insight.

Books by Cynthia Ozick

Trust
The Pagan Rabbi and Other Stories
Bloodshed and Three Novellas
Levitation: Five Fictions
Art & Ardor: Essays
The Cannibal Galaxy
The Messiah of Stockholm
Metaphor & Memory
The Shawl
What Henry James Knew and Other Essays on Writers
Fame & Folly: Essays
Portrait of the Artist as a Bad Character
The Puttermesser Papers
Quarrel & Quandary

Readers who want to learn more about Cynthia Ozick are encouraged to seek out some of the books that she has enjoyed:

The Longest Journey, Howards End, and *A Passage to India,* E. M. Forster
Washington Square, Henry James
Henry James, Leon Edel
Middlemarch, George Eliot
The Heart of the Matter, Graham Greene
The Importance of Being Earnest, Oscar Wilde
American Pastoral, Philip Roth
The stories of Anton Chekhov

GRACE PALEY

Two-time National Book Award Finalist Grace Paley was born in 1922 in New York City, the setting for many of her stories. The child of Jewish immigrants from Russia, she attended Hunter College and York University briefly, and sat in on a poetry class taught by W. H.

Auden. She wrote poetry exclusively until the age of thirty-three, when she began writing the stories included in her first collection, The Little Disturbances of Man, *published in 1959. Her second collection of stories,* Enormous Changes at the Last Minute, *was a Finalist for the 1975 National Book Award for Fiction and was followed by* Later the Same Day. *Her most recent collection,* The Collected Stories, *was a Finalist for the 1994 National Book Award, hailed by the Fiction Panel for its dazzling array of characters struggling "memorably over the conundrums of the human heart. . . . Mothers, ex-husbands, daughters, sons, fathers, old friends are visited and revisited with an artistry that lends a new poetry to the short story form." She has also published several collections of poetry, including* Leaning Forward *and* Begin Again: New and Collected Poems; Long Walks and Intimate Talks, *with illustrations by Vera B. Williams; and a collection of prose pieces,* Just As I Thought.

A longtime feminist and peace activist, Ms. Paley taught writing at Sarah Lawrence College for twenty-two years and at other institutions including the City College of New York, Dartmouth College, and Columbia University. She was the first New York State Author to have been appointed by the governor, and is a member of the Executive Board of PEN. Among many other honors are an award from the National Institute of Arts and Letters; a 1994 Jewish Cultural Achievement Award for Literary Arts; a 1993 Vermont Award for Excellence in the Arts; a 1992 REA Award for Short Stories; and the inaugural Edith Wharton Citation of Merit Award. She lives in Thetford, Vermont, with her husband, Robert Nichols.

DIANE OSEN: You've said that a person who isn't listening and doesn't pay attention won't ever be a writer. So I've been wondering: What were some of the stories that you listened to and that captured your attention as a child?

GRACE PALEY: I don't know that I heard stories so much as talking. I mean, there was a lot of talking going on in the house—mostly my father, with my mother throwing in a few sentences now and then.

My father was a doctor in the Bronx and he'd come home and he'd say, "Oh, something terrible happened," you know, or some painful or worrisome thing, or something funny, because he was a very funny guy. Those were the kind of things I would hear at the family supper table—we never said "dinner" unless we were talking about a big lunch. And then when there was company, there were a lot of heated political arguments and big fights of all kinds.

DO: I have the impression that your family was very political.

GP: My grandmother had five children, and for her the supper table was a pretty terrible place when they were kids. (Of course, this was in Russia in the town of Uzovka.) My father was a Socialist. One of my uncles was an Anarchist. My aunt was a Communist. My other aunt was a Zionist. And then there was one uncle who really was too young to argue, but not too young to act. He was killed in 1905 and my grandmother became a very solemn person. It was hard for her to see her children so mad at each other all the time. I lived with my grandmother, or she lived with us, as long as I lived home, and my aunt who was a Communist lived there most of the time too. And my father and mother were anti-Communist. I've always said that an extended family is wonderful for the children, but for adults it's not so great. As my father used to say, "One kitchen for two women? Forget it." But it wasn't only the kitchen.

DO: Did your family also read about the history and politics they fought over?

GP: My father was a great reader, and a serious reader of history. He had on his table books by Prescott and Gibbon and others. My mother was a reader too, but I'm not so much aware of what she read. After my father's evening office hours, which ran from six to eight, and after he made his night house calls, they would sit down together in the living room and read. They also listened to music a lot. They had a very big record collection; as my father became a middle-class man and earned money, he put it into classical records. I couldn't help but be interested in music, too; and when I was about fourteen or fifteen, in order to keep me from running wild, which it looked like I was going to do, they worked out with me a musical program based on the records we owned. Every other Friday I would have a musical hour at the house and I'd invite all my friends. Pretty soon a lot of kids began to come, not just my intimate friends, but other Bronx kids who had heard about it and came over. In fact, that's how I met the boy I married. He rang the doorbell one day and said, "Is this where they have music?"

DO: What place did reading have in your life as a child?

GP: Well, I think I read all the children's books that children read, but sometimes I'm very mixed up about whether my children read them, or if I read them. I remember *Heidi* and *Hans Brinker* and *The Secret Garden* and *Nobody's Girl* and *Nobody's Boy*. We went to the library a lot; we may have gone to the library even more than we read, because it was such a nice long walk carrying four, five books back and forth and talking to each other the way girls do. And then there was always the day you persuaded the librarian to give you an adult card.

DO: When did you first begin to write?

GP: My sister, who died two years ago at ninety, was much older than I am, and a very loving person. She was very excited when I wrote a poem every now and then, and that encouraged me a lot. And she must have read to me, too. But it wasn't until my adolescence that I began to write poetry. I had begun to read a lot of poetry by then, and it's what I really cared about. As I said, really I owe so much to my sister and even my aunt. When I look at my old books I see that I'd been given the Louis Untermeyer poetry anthology very early, and a book of Robinson Jeffers's poems for my sixteenth birthday. I was just crazy about this guy on his promontory in California with a gloomy view of the world, which I certainly didn't share at all. By the time I was in my later teens I was reading the prose that my generation read: James Joyce and Gertrude Stein and so forth. There was a point at which I thought that Joyce had used up all of the words in the English language and no one could ever say anything again. But it turned out not to be so. Anyway, I was writing poems by then, mostly love poems but some other kinds, too. And when Auden was on my mind I wrote poems in what I call "British." Some of them, like his, were political. I don't think my work was very good, actually, but that's what I did: I read poems and I wrote poems.

DO: In recalling your writing life, you've described your sudden discovery that you had two ears—a literary ear for making poems, which I suppose was your literary ear; and an ear for the language of your home and your neighborhood, for writing stories. What led you to that insight?

GP: I was trying to write a story and I guess that's how I really became aware of it, though I couldn't have put my finger on it for a good couple of years. I had begun in 1956 or '57 to write the stories that became a book in 1959 and to put words in other people's mouths. And as soon as it wasn't me speaking, as soon as I started letting other people talk and have ideas in their heads, another language, the language of these people, the language of my neighborhood and my home, came forward. And I realized that I had learned to use my other ear. I used to say that when you're a poet you speak to the world, and when you're a story writer you get the world to speak to you. But these are just ideas, not facts. And both require two ears.

DO: One of the themes of those first stories was ordinary women and men "at love," as you put it. What piqued your interest in that subject?

GP: I had lived among women all my life—my mother, my grandmother, my sister, my aunt, and the best girlfriends that I hung out with. I can say almost all of the names of my best girlfriends from the time I was five, and if I met them tomorrow I'd hug and kiss them. But I wasn't conscious of what I had in common with other grown women until I had my kids and met other women with kids in the park and playgrounds. They were all women in their twenties, all with kids, and a lot of them had been dumped by guys. This single-mother thing has come up more in the last ten, fifteen, twenty years, but even forty-five years ago there were a lot of single women raising kids, especially in Greenwich Village. I'd always liked kids so I was really interested in this whole multigenerational life that was happening to me.

You know, when you're teaching writing to teenagers, you realize that they think there's only one generation—theirs. They don't know how to write about either the generation that preceded them, or the one that hasn't yet followed them. I was like that too. So it was a great thing for me at that time in my life to suddenly enter a multigenerational life.

DO: How did living that multigenerational life, particularly at a time when there was relatively little interest in publishing fiction about lives like yours or your friends', shape your sense of yourself as a writer?

GP: Let's put it this way: I always had a pencil and paper in my pocket. And I was aware of myself always as a person who loved language, who thought poems for a long time and then began to think stories. But I never had a sense of myself as a writer. I mean, when I had to take care of the kids, I was taking care of the kids, and when I was writing, I was a writer. When I began to write I thought nobody would be interested in stories about ordinary women's lives, but I felt I had to proceed anyway. I just said, So nobody reads it, so it won't get published—so what? But what kept me going was that after I had written three stories, this guy came over whose kids I was babysitting, and it turned out he was a Doubleday editor. His wife had told him to read these three stories and he did. And when he came back the next week for his kids, he said, "Write me seven more and we'll publish your book," and he gave me $500, which was a lot of money. The truth of the matter is that I have the kind of nature which is too easy-going, so I might not have written seven more stories right away. So I know how people need encouragement, because of my good experience with Ken McCormack. And, I should add, Aaron Asher, who got them into saleable Meridian paper editions almost immediately.

DO: Storytelling in your work often takes the form of listening or illuminating, rather than explaining—a quality that also distinguishes the work of one of your favorite writers, Isaac Babel. When did you first discover his stories?

GP: I first read Babel [collected in *Red Cavalry, Tales of Odessa, Stories*] after my first book was published, maybe around 1960. And as soon as I began to read him, I felt at home with him; I always felt that he and I had the same great-grandfather—which was possible. Part of it was that he wrote in Russian, and my family spoke Russian with each other, mostly. His language is so clear and so direct and so unsentimental. And then the permission he gives to his characters to speak is wonderful. He's interested in them all, in two different ways. In some of his stories, like "Gedali," he says, See? This person is like me, we're the same, I'm a Jew too. And in others, like "My First Goose," he says, I'm not like that person at all, this Cossack is still a mystery to me. What he likes so much about the Cossacks is their toughness and their truthfulness; they don't lie about anything. But he is stunned by their brutality, even when it's on his side. In "My First Goose," for example, the way in which he has to prove himself as a man is to kill a goose. So with Babel, you see why people write—to try, at times, to understand someone who is not like them, and then at other times, to discover how others are just like them.

DO: The narrator of your "Conversation with my Father" says, "Everyone, real or invented, deserves the open destiny of life," and that kind of open-endedness characterizes Babel's stories as well as your own. Why does that particular narrative strategy appeal to you so strongly?

GP: A lot of short-story writers don't recognize that fact. I some-times feel that if their stories went on for another day, everything would change. And it's cruel, I think, for the writer to end a story this way—to leave the reader feeling that the story should have had one more day, because something would happen that would change everything. Now, maybe that's what they want to say, really, but I don't think so. I think it's just a technique of curtailing things and giving you a stomachache. I have always lived in my personal life with a sense of there being another day; I haven't felt at any time that nothing will happen anymore. Alice Munro is better at that than I am. There is always another day—not always a happier one (that's not the point). I mean, I'm almost eighty years old and I still feel that way, even about our terrifying world this year, 2001.

DO: Many of your stories, like Babel's as well, are just a couple of pages long. What made you decide to explore this very short form?

GP: I just wrote those stories the way I could; I didn't even think that anybody would consider them stories. But you always experi-ment; every story you write is an experiment, a search for some kind of form. You're always wondering, How can I tell this story? Do I have to bring in a lot of characters? If people had said to me, We hate these tiny short stories, I would have probably been sent back to think more about it, but nothing like that happened.

It's funny, but at one time I thought that some of these very short stories, like "Love" or "Mother," came to me whole. That is, that after I had gotten the first line, I didn't have an awful lot of work to do because the work had been done earlier, in my head. I had this practice of occasionally bringing in to my writing class early drafts of a story, to show them how terrible they can be. I wanted to give them courage, to show them that if you really are driven to tell the story, that if you have a longing to get it right and true, then you should keep going. On this one occasion I brought in an early draft of a very short story, "Mother." Well, it was so marked up that I realized I had done a lot more work on it than I had thought. I re-membered the story coming to me like an apple or a pear, but it wasn't true at all. It shows how you really don't know what the hell you're doing.

DO: Another aspect of your work that many critics and readers admire is the comic inventiveness of your language, and the way, in every story, that you crystallize a character's experience or emotion or memory into a literary epiphany.

GP: That's just a lucky discovery of the right words. All of a sudden I know the words, because I'm trying to know the character.

DO: One of the wonderful recurring characters that we also come to know in your books is Faith. What are some of the special pleasures of creating a character over decades?

GP: There is a certain pleasure, for a short-story writer, in having somebody you can depend on. For a novelist, what happens to the characters over time is one of the most important things in his or her book. But unless the people reappear every now and then, a short-story writer will miss that pleasure. The funny thing is, I wrote about Faith without any paying attention to time; if anybody ever wanted to really sit down and look at the stories about her, they'd see the kids were babies at the wrong time and grown up at the wrong time. That is, when I wanted them older I made them older, and when I wanted them younger, I made them younger. Luckily, nobody has looked at it that way—yet. I often say Faith works for me.

DO: What made you decide to write a second story about her in the first place?

GP: I guess what happened is that I got more and more interested in women and children, in my own generation, and Faith helped me see what was happening with them, and enabled me to get at least a few inches away from myself—and I needed to do that. I had to have someone else tell these stories; I might not have been truthful enough. My major idea about fiction and nonfiction is that when a story is told for the second time, it's fiction—no matter what. I've thought of that a lot, but I never thought that's what she was doing for me—that she was being my second teller.

DO: What are some of your favorite Faith stories?

GP: I don't know about favorites, but it was very important to me to write some of them. "Friends" is one of those. It was about the death of a friend of mine and all of us coming together to visit her. And it was also about our friendship and how it ended, in a way, for some of us. Now my friends are now under the impression that we actually went to visit our other friend together, but we never did. That was invented. Also "Zagrowsky Tells"—where Faith is looked at by another teller.

DO: The power of fiction!

GP: Yes, but it's also the *relief* of fiction. You can make it all up and improve on it and give people better lives than they had. When I wrote my first story, "Good-bye and Good Luck," I remember I was thinking very much about my aunt, who did not have such a successful life in the end. I wanted somehow to give her an independent life, so I changed her life entirely—and that's how you write a story sometimes. You start off with somebody and then you make them somebody else.

DO: The kind of independent life you wanted for your aunt is also the kind of life many of your characters aspire to and eventually achieve. How would you characterize the impact of feminism on your career?

GP: I wouldn't have a career without it. "Career" is a peculiar word. It implies going up or down. For a serious artist, it's all just plowing the wonderful field dead ahead. Career is the *world's* critical eye.

I was a feminist from the beginning, you know; it was just natural for me to think like a woman. It wasn't because I was badly treated by men at any particular point, although my feelings were hurt, from a very young age, by the mean remarks that were often made about women, even at home. And I wished, when I was a small girl, to be a boy so I could really get out there and play; I had a very tomboyish attitude. And as a teenager I didn't identify with my mother or my sister; I didn't see that they were suffering, although it turns out that they were seriously oppressed, each of them by her own men, and their historically accepting time. It wasn't until I was a little older and had kids that I saw how women were blamed for everything. I had a friend whose son became schizophrenic, and they said it was all her fault. And then I had a friend with an autistic child, and she was also told it was her fault. So I was lucky to begin writing at a time when the women's movement was starting to happen. It seemed very natural to feel part of it. And even though I was convinced that nobody would read my first book at all, I was committed to writing about women's lives—even when I wrote from a man's point of view.

DO: In your book *Just As I Thought*, you say that the child is the reason for life, and according to the narrator of your story "Debts," telling stories as simply as possible can save a life. What's the connection, for you, between the child and the story?

GP: Some women didn't like it at all that I said that about children. But on any level, the seed is the reason for the tree, and the tree for the seed—and that doesn't seem to me very anti-women. I mean, my sister had no children, but my children were one of the greatest reasons in her life for pleasure, for hope and interest in the future. That's not to say you have to have children, but the next generation is the reason for life. And in a way the child *has* to be in the story for me, because writing only about the parents, or about a single generation, is not interesting. It doesn't have enough back-and-forth, enough dialectical life. It might have enough psychology, but not enough history.

DO: It was right around the time you began publishing your stories, I think, that you became acquainted with the Friends' philosophy, and decided that you wanted not only to speak truth to power, but act truth to power. How did you accomplish that? And how has the relationship between your art and your politics evolved over the past forty years or so?

GP: When I began to write stories I thought, Gee, I haven't read anything about women like the women I know. People assumed immediately that I was writing in opposition to men and their lives and that was true in a way, but that wasn't my intention; my idea was to write as truthfully as I could against silence. Children were also on my mind; I noticed they seemed to be absent from other books. The story "Zagrowsky Tells" [about Faith's encounter with an bigoted white pharmacist from her old neighborhood, and his African-American grandson] was on my mind for at least five years before I even began to write it. But I didn't say, "Oh, I must get children into books," or, "It's time I wrote a story with a black child in it." I was just interested in how people lived and that's what I wrote about.

When the Friends talk about speaking truth to power and acting truth to power, that means using your whole self to say what you believe and to accept the consequences. It means taking actions, like the civil disobedience that we were involved in in those days, and probably will be again, from the looks of things. It's a way of always *intervening*—a nice expression I learned, but I've been doing it. And I'll tell you a story.

A young woman we know was telling us recently that she works in a nice shop where the people are okay but the clothes are expensive—because the owners are Jewish. Well, my husband wanted me to let it go, but the thing is you can never let anything like that slide. So I took her hand and said, "You know, you're really hurting my feelings with what you just said. *All* the shopkeepers in Hanover are trying to make a profit." At that point her father said, "She didn't say anything," but the daughter said, "No, I *did* say something. I did." And she took my hand and said, "I'll never say that again." This is a small story in a small place.

You can never let things go—and not just in private life. You have to respond in public life. And I think that that has always been the writer's task, in a way. Without knowing it, the writer writes in response to some idea or event or action or lack of action. We write about what oppresses us, about what hurts our hearts. But I don't think the writer is more of a citizen than anybody else in this country; every person has the obligation of citizenship. We all have to answer for our minute in history.

BOOKS BY GRACE PALEY
> *The Little Disturbances of Man*
> *Enormous Changes at the Last Minute*
> *Later the Same Day*
> *Leaning Forward*
> *Long Walks and Intimate Talks*
> *Begin Again: New and Collected Poems*
> *The Collected Stories*
> *Just As I Thought*

Readers interested in learning more about Grace Paley may want to read some of the books that have shaped her writing life:
> The Bible
> Mother Goose
> *The Collected Stories,* Isaac Babel
> *Mrs. Dalloway* and *To the Lighthouse,* Virginia Woolf
> *Dubliners,* James Joyce

Linda Pastan

*Linda Pastan, a two-time Finalist for the National Book Award and a
former Poet Laureate of Maryland, was born and raised in New York
City. As an undergraduate at Radcliffe College, she won the* Mademoiselle *magazine poetry contest; after graduation in 1954, she
earned two master's degrees, in library science and English, and had
three children before resuming her career as a poet. She won her first
National Book Award nomination in 1982, for* PM/AM: New and

Selected Poems, *and her second in 1998, for* Carnival Evening: New and Selected Poems, 1968–1998. *She has published nine other collections of poetry, including the recent* The Last Uncle. *A staff member of the Bread Loaf Writers' Conference for twenty years, she has also taught at American University, and has given readings of her work across the country. Among the many awards she has received are the Dylan Thomas Award, the Alice Fay di Castagnola Award, the Bess Hokin Prize from* Poetry *magazine, the Maurice English Award, and a Pushcart Prize. She lives in Potomac, Maryland, with her husband.*

Linda Pastan's poems have long inspired readers to explore the places in their lives where, as she puts it, "fact and fable intersect." Praised by the National Book Award's poetry judges as "exquisite miniatures of twentieth-century life," the poems in Carnival Evening *are "capacious because her passionate attentiveness to the smallest fact of experience excludes nothing, and audacious because the simplest events seen through the prism of her language bring into focus the refractions of grief."*

DIANE OSEN: Many of your best-known poems are about the forms and functions of memory. When you think back today on your life as a child, what do you remember most vividly?

LINDA PASTAN: I suppose I remember being lonely and being saved by books. I didn't have any brothers or sisters; my father was a surgeon and my mother dedicated her life to making him comfortable. She drove him to the hospital; she worked in his office; she laid out the clothes he was going to wear. And I went to a school called Fieldston—actually, a lot of poets have gone there—that was far from the part of the Bronx where I lived, so I didn't have friends in the neighborhood.

But my parents had crowded bookcases, and there were all those characters in all those books; I guess I felt they were substitute siblings. What I remember best about my childhood is sitting on the floor and reading compulsively while my parents kept saying, Why don't you go outside and play? I read absolutely without discrimination; I just worked my way through the shelves. I read history books, I read cookbooks. I think I read *The Grapes of Wrath* when I was eleven years old.

DO: That must have made quite an impression.

LP: It terrified me, but I couldn't stop reading. And I read poetry, too. There was a beautiful little volume by Emily Dickinson, bound in leather, that I often kept with me. And when I got older, there was a *Little Treasury of Modern Poetry* edited by Oscar Williams, with wonderful locket-sized pictures of the poets looking very young and vulnerable. I remember reading books by Edna St. Vincent Millay and Elizabeth Barrett Browning and Tennyson—his "Crossing the Bar" was one of my favorite poems.

DO: When did you first begin composing your own poetry?

LP: Well, between, say, the ages of nine and eleven, I began to feel that reading wasn't quite enough. It was as though all the authors were writing monologues, and what I needed was to be part of a dialogue. And so I began by imitating the poets whose poems I liked. I must have thought of myself as a new young Housman: I was twelve years old, writing about early death, and always in strict rhyme and meter. I wrote some short stories, too, but from the beginning it was poetry that interested me most.

Later, at Radcliffe, where I went to college, there were few writing classes; we read and studied the great literature of the past. I don't regret that at all; in any case reading is almost always the best education for a writer. And I did write constantly—mostly about unhappy love, as I recall. I was published for the first time when I won the *Mademoiselle* magazine poetry contest. The only poetry writing course I even knew of was given by Archibald MacLeish, but it was offered the year after I got married—I had married five days after my twenty-first birthday, before my senior year—and I didn't feel that I could be a good wife, a good scholar, and write poetry, too. I didn't even choose to write my undergraduate thesis about a poet. I wrote it on the unfinished novels of Nathaniel Hawthorne—a very strange subject for a young, beginning writer, since it was all about the failed work of a great writer at the end of his life. I wonder if Hawthorne's pain influenced my own silence later: That possibility didn't occur to me until just this moment.

At any rate, after I graduated my father insisted that I have some practical way of making my own living, so I got a master's degree in library science. That was about the most miserable year of my life. The following year I went to Brandeis University and got another master's degree, this time in English literature. I studied there with J. V. Cunningham, a brilliant, underappreciated poet, and wrote poems just for him, as part of a private tutorial. It was incredible training in formal verse. But then, after only two years at Brandeis, we had to leave Boston. My husband had gotten a medical internship at Yale, and in those years a woman more or less automatically went to whatever place was best for her husband's career. Yale didn't take graduate students part time, or so I was told, and since by that time I had a baby, moving to New Haven was the death knell for the writing that I had done so much of at Brandeis. Instead, I had another baby. With an intern husband always at work or asleep, I became bogged down in domestic life. Poetry—which was so important to me—is what I just let go. For all sorts of reasons that I still don't altogether understand, I more or less stopped writing for the next ten years.

DO: What brought you back?

LP: It was 1965. I was thirty-three years old and had just had my third and final child when *Necessities of Life,* by Adrienne Rich, appeared. In some ways it was the title that engaged me, because I was finally starting to realize that, after ten years of silence, poetry was one of my own life's necessities. I had been aware of Adrienne Cecile Rich (as we thought of her then) for years; she had been a few years ahead of me at Radcliffe and she had taken MacLeish's poetry writing course. Over the years, I had read her poems as they came out in *The New Yorker,* and always felt this terrible ambivalence about her work: real pleasure, along with real pain that she was doing what I had always felt I should be trying to do.

Her book was one of the triggers for my own writing. For ten years, I had been silent even though I knew that writing poems was the one thing I should be doing. I always felt vaguely guilty about this, and I did complain about it a lot. Finally my husband, who is very patient, said that he was tired of hearing what a good poet I would have been if I hadn't married him. The two of us sat down together and made a schedule, hired a babysitter for a few hours each morning, and I started to write again. For the first six months, I wrote a new poem practically every day. All that compressed energy from those ten silent years, all the things that had happened to me during that time, just came bursting out. I've never had a period of writing that productive again.

DO: What was it about that book that inspired you?

LP: Well, I was inspired partly by her style, which helped free me from all the formal and rather rigidly metrical poems that I had always written in the past; I think it was just the change that I needed at that time. And there also was a kind of organized casualness to her voice in this book. It was clear, it was intelligent, and it was engaged. And she had a wonderful feeling for metaphor and the places that metaphor could take you. Metaphor has always been my major interest; it's what I'm most drawn to in poetry.

There are many poems that I really love in this book—for instance, "Like This Together." I particularly remember being taken by the lines, "Rooms cut in half / hanging like flayed carcasses, / Their old roses in rags, / famous streets have forgotten / where they were going." And in another poem called "In the Woods," she writes, " 'Difficult, ordinary happiness,' / no one nowadays believes in you." The poems here are preoccupied with difficult ordinary happiness, though this isn't something she will write about much later on, but it has always been something that's preoccupied me. The poems in this book are only very subliminally political, so different from the very angry and very highly feminist poems that she would write later. I'm less interested in overtly political poetry, though I often admire it—particularly Rich's.

DO: What about James Wright? How did his work come to shape your writing life?

LP: The influence James Wright had on me was very different from the influence of Rich. *Shall We Gather at the River* came out several years after *Necessities of Life*, and it led me immediately to *The Branch Will Not Break*. I was well on the way to my own first book by this time, and I wasn't looking to be influenced. In any case, I can't be entirely rational about the effect Wright had on me; I simply fell in love with his poems. They have an emotional charge that is breathtaking in its simplicity, and they made me confront the problem of locating the line between genuine sentiment and sentimentality. He dared to go dangerously close to that line, as if it were an electric wire and had a charge that lent energy to the work but could burn if it were actually touched. Wright gave me the courage to dare to fail. I had always felt that I had to hold back somewhat, and here was someone who came so close but knew just when to stop—or didn't know when to stop but just stopped somehow. And of course his famous line, "I have wasted my life," may have affected me in ways I didn't suspect. I still feel the same way about Wright's poems all these years afterward; they always bring me close to tears.

DO: Is that line between sentiment and sentimentality something you still wrestle with?

LP: Yes. And I probably stay further away from it than I might, perhaps because I'm more afraid of failure than I think I am. It's something that poets who write about the kinds of subjects I write about do have to be careful of, though. For example, I'm still writing so many poems about death—I'm not sure why—and I don't want them to go over the edge.

DO: No matter what your subject, your poems have an extraordinary immediacy which comes, I think, from your interest in "the mystery of the every day," as you once put it, and from the voices of your speakers, who so often address the reader directly and seemingly without artifice. How have these features of your poems evolved over the years?

LP: I think my voice hasn't really changed very much since 1965, when I started writing again and started thinking of myself as a writer. I'm not sure why that is, and I'm not sure it's a good thing. But if somebody looked at my poems without knowing which book they were from, I imagine it would be hard for them to say in which decade they were written. I don't think the form of my work has changed very much, either; I've always written a rather loose but controlled free verse lyric, with the occasional formal poem thrown in. What I write about, however, has changed as my life has changed, for my poetry has always been immersed in my life. I used to write poems about childbirth and small children, and then there were a lot of poems about adolescence, about children leaving home. Now my poems seem to concern growing old, and although the threat of loss has always been one of my major themes, loss has now become more than simply a threat.

Often people who read or hear my work feel that they really know me, particularly since the names of family members in the poems are the same as the names of my real family. What people often don't realize is that the first person "I" in my work is not necessarily me: As I've said before, it's a fraternal rather than an identical twin. But I generally do feel that same kind of immediacy you ask about with poems I love, even when they are quite formal poems. I think one of the hallmarks of true poetry *is* that mysterious, almost umbilical connection between the poem and the reader. Certainly I feel it with the poems by Rich and Wright that I've been talking about.

DO: What about your persona poems? How did they evolve?

LP: As you know, I write quite often in the voice of Eve and in the voice of Penelope, two women with whom I feel a very real connection. When I spoke earlier about trying to get close to the line between genuine sentiment and sentimentality, I remembered my earliest Penelope poem, which was in my first book, *A Perfect Circle of Sun*. It was written as a poem about a woman standing at a window, longing for her husband or lover who had gone off somewhere. When I finished the poem it felt self-indulgent somehow. And then all of a sudden it occurred to me that the poem was really about Penelope, not about me. Or perhaps about both of us. I gave it the title "Penelope," but didn't change another thing. This provided exactly the distance, the coolness, you might say, that the poem had needed. That's just one example of how writing in the voice of a persona, a Penelope or an Eve, can allow one to do things one might not successfully do, using the first person singular.

DO: In your poem "Vermilion," you write about revision being "the purest form of love." How is it that you fell in love with revision? And can you perhaps describe the process that has led you to be called "a master of compression"?

LP: That's a really interesting question. It's not that I want to be a so-called "master of compression." I'd love to write *War and Peace;* I'd love to write long, narrative poems. But instead I start with a lot of material, a kind of hunk of marble somehow excreted onto the page, and my job seems to be to chisel at it and chisel at it until everything that doesn't belong has been removed.

For example, I have an early poem called "Knots," from *Aspects of Eve,* my second book. It began as a poem about my great-grandmother saving string, which she tied around her finger to help her remember things, and it ended with her coffin being tied up with string. It was a very neat and tidy poem, but I just didn't think it was very good. And whoever ties a coffin up with string anyway? I went back into the poem, more or less free-associating, until I got all this stuff: a long, long page about sailors' knots and string and

Rumpelstiltskin—all kinds of material. And then I started paring it down again until all I had left was another small poem, this time with sailors' knots and shoestring, and no great-grandmother at all. It turned out to be a poem about wanting to flee domesticity, which is not at all where it began.

This business of not knowing where a poem is going when you begin it is something I started thinking about after reading an essay by William Stafford called "Writing the Australian Crawl." He says you must trust the poem and follow it where it wants to take you, along the way learning things you didn't even know you knew. Reading this, and getting to know Stafford personally, changed the way I wrote. I didn't wait anymore until I had an "idea." Instead I would start with an image, or a feeling, or even a sound, and see where it led. Stafford is also one of the poets I turn to when I have so-called "writer's block," because there is something about his voice that makes writing feel natural, feel easy. It's not that what he has to say is simple, but something about the simplicity of the diction draws you right in.

DO: You also write a lot about works of art, as in "Woman Holding a Balance," one of my favorite poems of yours.

LP: If I had my choice, I would have been a painter, not a poet; that, to me, would be the ultimate thing to be. But though I have no painterly skills, I do have a visual imagination, and maybe that's why I have always written a lot of poems based on works of art. It also helps that I live outside Washington, D.C., where there are so many wonderful museums and traveling art shows. I know that there are people who maintain that one shouldn't write poems about art, or for that matter poems about poetry, but I can't help it. I'm very emotionally moved by painting and sculpture, and when I'm moved, poems seem to come. I wrote the particular poem you mention after waiting two hours to get into a Vermeer show at the National Gallery of Art. I love the domesticity of Vermeer's subjects. One of my themes has always been the dangers lurking beneath ordinary domestic surfaces, and it's the incredibly lit domestic surfaces of Vermeer, beneath which so many things lurk, that totally fascinate me.

DO: That's something you write about in "Who Is It Accuses Us": "I tell you household gods / are jealous gods."

LP: Yes. Someone once said to me that I hid in the safety of the family, and the idea that anyone could think a family was a safe place absolutely floored me. I think that domestic life—where you have so many loved hostages around you—is particularly dangerous. And the surfaces of my life have become even more fragile as I've gotten older and loss has become an everyday fact. My friends have started to die, aunts and uncles and parents have disappeared. I think that's why falling leaves, which disappear right outside my window, make their way into so many of my poems. I always say that I'm not going to allow any more leaves into my work, and then there they are.

DO: Writing about landscape, Barry Lopez has suggested that it "urges us to come around to an understanding of ourselves." You, too, write often about the natural world, most notably about trees, as you just said, and small animals. How has your imagination been shaped by the landscape you live in?

LP: I live in the middle of six acres of oak forest—you can't see any other houses from here—and it's a quiet but nevertheless sumptuous landscape. My husband was once offered a job in California, and I said, I can't go there: If I don't have four really distinct seasons, I'm not going to be able to write poems. Each time it snows it feels to me as if it's the first time it's ever snowed; in fall it feels as if the leaves have never before turned color. My imagination is completely energized, over and over again, by the annual changes outside my windows and by what these changes are emblematic of.

DO: When I think of leaves in your poems, I think of "Wind Chill," where you describe "small leaves clicking / in their coffins of ice."

LP: That's one of my favorite poems, actually. And one of my favorite forms of poetry is a small, descriptive lyric that has a lot going on under its surfaces.

DO: What are you working on now? And what do you see down the road?

LP: I have just put together a new book, *The Last Uncle,* which Norton will publish in 2002. Meanwhile, as always, I sit down at my desk every morning and try to write poems, one at a time. It is as if every new poem is my first poem. I have always felt that all poetry, no matter what its ostensible subject, is basically political. Evil, I wrote in a poem called "Instructions to the Reader," is "simply a grammatical error: / a failure to leap / the precipice / between 'he'/ and I." That is, evil is often a failure of the imagination, and the imagination is like a muscle that reading poems can strengthen. As long as I continue to believe this, I will continue to try and write. I live a very isolated life out here in the woods. My husband leaves early in the morning and comes back in the evening; my children are more or less scattered. And so books, once again, have become my most important companions. When I think about what's down the road, what I see are the final losses. So I don't really plan except for the next line of whatever poem I'm working on.

BOOKS BY LINDA PASTAN
>
> *A Perfect Circle of Sun*
> *Aspects of Eve*
> *The Five Stages of Grief*
> *Waiting for My Life*
> *PM/AM: New and Selected Poems*
> *A Fraction of Darkness*
> *The Imperfect Paradise*
> *Heroes in Disguise*
> *An Early Afterlife*
> *Carnival Evening*
> *The Last Uncle*

Readers who want to learn more about Linda Pastan are encouraged to explore some of the books that have changed her life:

> *A Little Treasure of Modern Poetry*, Oscar Williams (editor)
> *A Pocket Book of Verse*
> *The Branch Will Not Break* and *Shall We Gather at the River*, James Wright
> *Necessities of Life*, Adrienne Rich
> *Writing the Australian Crawl*, William Stafford

KATHERINE PATERSON

Katherine Paterson, a two-time Winner of the National Book Award for The Master Puppeteer *and* The Great Gilly Hopkins, *was born in China to a family of Christian missionaries. She moved to the United States at the start of World War II, later earning a bachelor's degree from King College, and master's degrees from the Presbyterian School of Education and Union Theological Seminary in New York.*

The author of more than two dozen books, including fourteen novels for young people, Ms. Paterson worked as a missionary in Japan for four years before becoming a writer. The Great Gilly Hopkins *is her fifth novel, published in 1978. Set in the South, this seriocomic tale traces the struggles of a seemingly tough foster child to find love and acceptance from others, as well as herself. Reviewing the novel, critics agreed with M. Sarah Smedman that it powerfully "dramatize[s] a young protagonist's encounter with the mysteries of grace and love," as well as the author's "commitment to the young reader's right to an absorbing story." The book was adapted for the stage by her son David in 1997.*

In 1998, Ms. Paterson received the Hans Christian Andersen Medal, the most distinguished international award for children's literature, and was named a Library Lion by the New York Public Library. Among her other awards are two Newbery Medals for her novels Bridge to Terabithia *and* Jacob Have I Loved, *as well as the Scott O'Dell Award for Historical Fiction and honors from the American Library Association, the Library of Congress, and* School Library Journal. *To date, her books have been published in twenty-five languages; her most recent book,* The Invisible Child, *was published in 2001.*

Katherine Paterson lives in Vermont with her husband, the Rev. John B. Paterson, with whom she has written two books, Consider the Lilies: Plants of the Bible *and* Images of God. *They have four children and seven grandchildren.*

DIANE OSEN: I know you grew up in a Christian missionary family in China, and I've read that you'd moved fifteen times by the time you were fifteen, and often felt different from other kids your own age. How do you think these factors shaped your early experiences as both a reader and a writer?

KATHERINE PATERSON: Reading was where I could always find friends. I learned to trust books, and to love books, and to find a great deal of comfort from books when I was quite young. And although I didn't think of myself as a writer or write very much as a child, I certainly did what writers have to do: look at life from the outside in. At the same time, I was very conscious of my own feelings. I often say that I don't have a very good memory for events, but I have a good emotional memory.

DO: What kinds of books did you read during those years?

KP: We had mostly English books in China, because English children's books were much more evident in those days; we hadn't really come into the golden age of American children's books yet. And we had a lot of fairy tales, as well as Bible stories and the King James Bible itself. Then, as I got older, I discovered Dickens. When I was reading *A Tale of Two Cities,* I could hardly wait to get home from school. I wouldn't even take off my coat; I would just lie down on the living room floor and read.

DO: Were you thinking at all then about becoming a writer?

KP: No, no, not at all. I always hesitate to tell children that, because most of them sit there wide-eyed and eager, knowing that God has called them to be writers by the time they're eight years old. And for most of my writer friends, that was true; they knew quite early on that they wanted to be writers. But I had no notion of it.

DO: When did you start to write?

KP: I was asked to write my first book. I had a professor at graduate school who stopped me in the hall one day and said, Have you ever thought of becoming a writer? I was just flabbergasted. I said I wouldn't want to add another mediocre writer to this world. Being a glorious failure didn't scare me at all, but being just mediocre did.

What I heard her say was, If you're not willing to be mediocre, you'll never be anything at all. I think that's a very important lesson to learn, because people always want guarantees that they're going to be wonderful. But there's no way of knowing you're good, if you don't dare to be mediocre.

I pooh-poohed the idea of writing as politely as I could; but after I had come back from four years of working in Japan, and had gotten another master's degree, and had gotten married, she recommended me to write a book for the Presbyterian church for fifth and sixth graders. I wrote a book called *Who Am I?*, which has been revised and reissued, and which is propaganda. But good propaganda, I think.

DO: What do you mean by "good" propaganda?

KP: When people want me to write didactic novels, I say, No, I know the difference between propaganda and novels, because I've written propaganda. And there's nothing wrong with good propaganda; you think you have something to share and you share it. But with a novel, you begin with your own questions, doubts, and fears; you're not starting out with any answers. That's why I love stories, because there is always a transaction between reader and writer; you can't dictate the meaning. You can just lay the story out and invite the reader to enter in and make his or her own meaning.

DO: When did you first encounter *Cry, the Beloved Country?* And how did reading it change your writing life?

KP: The book was actually read to me. I was working one summer at a Presbyterian conference center in North Carolina near Asheville and I got to know Mary, who is still one of my dearest friends. She had grown up in what was then called the Belgian Congo and had discovered *Cry, the Beloved Country.* She read it aloud to me, and she knew how those African sounds worked. It was a very sensual experience for me, just lying on my bed with my eyes closed, with this beautiful voice reading to me properly. I'm sure that's one reason it was so powerful for me, because I wasn't stumbling through the pronunciations on my own.

What absolutely threw me about that book, and what still haunts me, is that it made me realize what the American South was. I had lived in the segregated South since I was eight years old and had taken it for granted that's the way things were—and then suddenly, by reading about another country that was taking injustice for granted, I realized what we were doing in my own country. And it was a heartbreaking experience for me. I remember just crying and crying and crying when it dawned on me. And so it was a life-changing book for me in a way that I think very few books are.

DO: What did you think of the novel when you reread it recently?

KP: I'd forgotten how didactic Alan Paton was. I mean didactic in a good sense, but not in a sense that we usually want to see in a novel. He wants to let us know the pain of his country, and the terrible suffering and fear. Fear is the thing that came through to me most strongly—that so many of the characters, black and white, were acting out of fear, and how all of us were acting out of fear in the South. I was astounded how often I just burst into tears while reading it, and how, despite its flaws—and I think there are flaws there—the power of the story is so overwhelming. I'm going to burst into tears again.

DO: Toward the end of *Cry, the Beloved Country,* Kumalo discovers, as he puts it to a friend, that " 'love and kindness can pay for pain and suffering.' " That same theme resonates in your work, especially in *The Great Gilly Hopkins.* How did you come to write that novel?

KP: In 1975 a planeload of Cambodian children appeared at Dulles Airport with no papers whatsoever. A local social service agency was asked to find people to be temporary foster parents for these kids, and they asked us if we would take two brothers for two weeks. I thought, Four kids, six kids, what's the difference? And besides, I thought these boys would be so lucky to come to the only home in the greater Washington area where the mother knows how to cook rice.

And so we picked up our two brothers and bought bunk beds, and the first couple of days everything was fine—and then everything began falling apart. I felt frustrated and unhappy and I was saying to myself when problems arose, I can't deal with this problem, they're only going to be here for two weeks. And in the next breath I was saying, Thank God they're only going to be here for two weeks. And it finally dawned on me that I was saying these kids are disposable. As soon as I heard what I was really saying, I was horrified. I had to think how I would behave if I felt the world regarded me as disposable. And I thought I would be furious.

DO: When you published the novel in 1978, Gilly was something of an anomaly—much edgier than most of the fictional characters that young readers found appealing then. How have readers responded to her over the years?

KP: I thought *Gilly Hopkins* was going to be a funny book. I meant for it to be a funny book, and then it just got weird on me. Of course, it's read by all manner of children, and the children who have a fairly safe environment and who love their homes are just furious that she doesn't get to go back to Trotter. But the children who have had a very hard life say, That's not the way it is. Anger is the basic thing going here. And what children who can identify with that kind of anger get is a deep comfort from finding it in a book—and also the hope that there might be something beyond that.

Initially nobody attacked me on the racial issues in the book; all they attacked me for was fairly mild cursing. I got a letter from some kids the other day and it says, Everybody knows the word [nigger] that Gilly wants you to think of when she writes that poem to her teacher; don't you think it's terrible to put that word in a book for children? And, yes, I think it's shocking. But my thought was, I don't want her to be mischievous; I want her to be truly malevolent. I want her behavior to be so bad that nobody can excuse it, because you can't perceive her as truly a troubled child unless she does something that shocks you. Because when you're that wounded, what you do is strike out against someone to make yourself feel better; you're not so bad if there's somebody worse than you are. And the character thinks that she can do something that's really very malicious by using that word.

I remember one woman just going at me, and she said, What did your father think of such a book? knowing that my father was a very conservative Presbyterian. And I said, Well, of all of my books *The Great Gilly Hopkins* is his favorite, but then he's read the story of the prodigal son. Which was a mean thing for me to say, but he did understand what the story was about. It's very sad to me that many Christians don't understand it. They think that a Christian book is nice. They don't understand that Christians deal with life-and-death, hell-and-heaven issues. And sin is a very important part of what we have to say.

DO: You've said that it was chance that led you to write for young audiences initially. What inspired you to continue?

KP: I think it was the wonderful experience of working with my editor, Virginia Buckley, that convinced me. I've had the same editor for all my novels. And I've continued to write what I want to write, and the people who want to read it are usually between the ages of ten and fourteen. That's not to say I write a book for ten- to fourteen-year-olds; that's the way I write, and they're my natural audience. I'm one of the few people in the world who is fortunate enough to have found out what it is she's supposed to be doing. And not only am I allowed to do it, but I'm honored for doing it.

DO: What do you see as your responsibilities toward your readers?

KP: People want me to say that I'm thinking of my audience all the time. Actually, I'm not. I'm trying to write the best story I know how to write. And I want it to be true, but my truth will always be a partial truth. That's why we all need one another.

I have been thinking lately about the responsibilities of those of us who write for children, because it seems to me that in the last few years there has been a whole raft of books that are just so depressing that I think, What child in the world would I ever hand this book to? It's not that I think that when you write for children you say, Okay, time to tack the hope on. But I don't quite understand why it is we want to give children total despair, because I don't think that's realistic either.

The debates that we've had recently about the film *Life Is Beautiful* are very significant. There are people who say, How can you have a funny movie about the Holocaust? It's not a funny movie— but you see the awfulness of the Holocaust in a whole new way because you see it through the eyes of a person who's determined to love life. And that makes the Holocaust all the more awful, because he's a man who should have lived and who, every day that he lived, gave joy to others. If you only see the awfulness, then you're destroyed by the despair and you're no good to anybody. But if you believe that there's something worth living for and that life essentially is beautiful, then you can work for that in a way that a person who has no hope cannot begin to.

BOOKS BY KATHERINE PATERSON
The Sign of the Chrysanthemum
Of Nightingales That Weep
The Master Puppeteer
Bridge to Terabithia
The Great Gilly Hopkins
Angels and Other Strangers
Jacob Have I Loved
The Crane Wife (translation)
Rebels of the Heavenly Kingdom
Come Sing, Jimmy Jo
The Tongue-Cut Sparrow (translation)
Park's Quest
The Spying Heart (retelling)
The Tale of the Mandarin Ducks
Lyddie
The Smallest Cow in the World
The King's Equal
Who Am I?
Flip-Flop Girl

A Midnight Clear: Stories for the Christmas Season
A Sense of Wonder
Jip, His Story
The Angel and the Donkey (retelling)
Marvin's Best Christmas Present Ever
Parzival
Images of God (with John Paterson)
Consider the Lilies: Plants of the Bible (with John Paterson)
Celia and the Sweet, Sweet Water
Preacher's Boy
The Wide-Awake Princess
The Field of the Dogs
Marvin One Too Many
The Invisible Child (essays for adults)
The Same Stuff as Stars

Readers who want to learn more about Katherine Paterson are encouraged to seek out some of the books that have changed her writing life:

Cry, the Beloved Country, Alan Paton
Kristin Lavransdatter, Sigrid Undset
Clear Light of Day, Anita Desai
Silence, Shusaku Endo
Emma, Jane Austen
Poems, Gerard Manley Hopkins

ROBERT STONE

Multiple National Book Award honoree Robert Stone was born in Brooklyn, New York, in 1937 and raised on the Upper West Side of Manhattan. After suffering a crisis of faith he dropped out of Saint Ann's, a Catholic high school in Manhattan, and enlisted in the navy, eventually serving as senior enlisted journalist on a scientific mission in Antarctica. Following a brief stint as a copyboy at New York's Daily News *and as a student at New York University, he married and moved to New Orleans, where he worked variously as an actor, en-*

cyclopedia salesman, and coffee factory worker, among other occupations. The city was to serve as the setting of his first novel, the William Faulkner Award–winning A Hall of Mirrors. *Beginning in 1962, however, he was able to devote more time to his writing as a Stegner Fellow at Stanford University, where he joined the social circle known as the Merry Pranksters and immortalized in Tom Wolfe's* Electric Kool-Aid Acid Test. *After working as a freelance writer in London, Hollywood, and Saigon, he published* Dog Soldiers, *the Winner of the 1975 National Book Award for Fiction. His next novel,* A Flag for Sunrise, *was also nominated for a National Book Award, as well as a Pulitzer Prize, a National Book Critics Circle Award, and the PEN/Faulkner Award.* Children of Light *was published in 1986, followed by* Outerbridge Reach, *which gained him his third National Book Award nomination;* Damascus Gate, *published in 1998, was also nominated for a National Book Award. In addition to* Bear and His Daughter, *a collection of short stories nominated for a Pulitzer Prize, he wrote the screenplay for the film* WUSA, *based on his* A Hall of Mirrors, *and cowrote the screenplay for* Who'll Stop the Rain, *based on* Dog Soldiers. *Among other honors, he has received the American Academy and Institute of Arts and Letters Award, the John Dos Passos Prize for Literature, and a Mildred and Harold Strauss Living Award. Currently Chairman of the PEN/Faulkner Award Foundation and a member of the faculty at Yale University, he has taught writing at colleges and universities including Johns Hopkins University, New York University, Amherst College, and Princeton University. He lives with his wife, Janice, in New York City.*

Robert Stone's *masterful* Outerbridge Reach *is the story of Owen Browne, a yacht broker who has never sailed alone, but who nonetheless enters a solo, round-the-world race to escape from "a cheap modern culture he despises, in search of honor, risk, meaning, manhood and God," said the 1992 National Book Award fiction judges. "It's as if Melville and Conrad had gone to sea with William Blake." His 1998 novel* Damascus Gate *was likewise praised by the National Book Award's panelists as "a novel of ideas masquerading as an action thriller" from "a novelist equally at home with cultural apocalypse and individual affections."*

DIANE OSEN: In preparing for our interview, I was struck by something that you told another interviewer several years ago—that being raised by a schizophrenic had given you a tremendous advantage, as you put it, in understanding the relationship between language and reality. How do you remember perceiving that relationship as a child? And when did books begin to enter the equation for you?

ROBERT STONE: It wasn't until I began to think about what fiction really was that I began to connect it to things like the schizophrenic condition; it wasn't something that occurred to me as a child. And books didn't enter that equation until much later. But I was aware, as a child, of trying to make out the difference between what was really going on and what my mother thought was going on. When you live with somebody who is delusional, you sometimes have to serve as a kind of interpreter: You take the world as you perceive it and you render it in a way that makes it comprehensible for the person you're translating for. And you become adept at understanding what *they* mean, even if it might not make sense to another person, because you know what they are experiencing. So I did get into the question, at a very early stage, of whether words have an absolute meaning, or whether they have a relative meaning—the old Platonic problem. It's not a complex philosophical question, really. I mean, everybody, in a way, bends language to their own particular meaning, but eventually we bring it into conformity with everybody else's language. Schizophrenics don't always do this; they maintain a private code in the way that children do. And if you have to deal with somebody who goes on having that kind of private code, the questions you ask yourself about that language and how it can exist are questions that are of interest to you later when you're writing.

DO: When did you start to write? And what inspired you?

RS: Being read to, either at boarding school or at home with my mother, was one of the entertainments available to me as a child.

And as soon as I found out that these entertainments were in books that I could read myself, I started wanting to fabricate entertainments of that sort myself. A lot of what captured my attention early on was the science fiction that I heard on the radio and read in the comic books and magazines that were everywhere then, with their spectacular and sometimes lurid covers. I also read a lot of illustrated science fiction books and Ray Bradbury's stories. A lot of the things that I tried to write were also in the vein of science fiction. The only aspect of school I was successful in was writing compositions, and to some extent, doing Latin translations—and that was what I enjoyed doing.

By the time I was in high school, I had genuine literary ambitions and had discovered the world of serious fiction, but I really couldn't see myself as an inventor of stories or novels. I wanted to be a newspaperman. I joined the navy without finishing high school and was a radio operator for a while. Then I took the test for journalist—the navy has a formal rating of "journalist"—and they assigned me to the 1958 Antarctic Operation, Deep Freeze Three. I had a very interesting time doing that, and it gave me the opportunity, I think, to work for the *Daily News* at night after I got out of the navy. But the *Daily News* was a very conservative outfit, and I was just not the kind of guy they were interested in promoting into their higher ranks. In a way I was lucky that I didn't have more success as a journalist, because it would have sidetracked me considerably: I wouldn't have taken as seriously my writing courses at NYU, and I wouldn't have pursued the opportunity to go to Stanford University as a Stegner Fellow. But luckily I burned my bridges, because by then I really wanted to become a writer of fiction.

DO: I know that Hemingway's *The Sun Also Rises* is one of your favorite books, and that you believe an important goal for any writer should be to "write well and truly," as Hemingway himself might have phrased it. When did you discover that novel?

RS: I think I happened on *The Sun Also Rises* when I was in high school, and I remember finding the language in it bubbling like champagne. The wonderful sense of life that he brings to bear makes you want to live that life and want to write that way. In that sense Hemingway was tremendously inspiring to generations of American writers. There is maybe something a little bit false about his fiction, but it's a wonderful fantasy of beautiful men and beautiful women talking beautiful language and living wonderful lives. And if they are sad and existentially melancholy, if they are overshadowed by a sense of tragedy, it does not daunt them. They proceed to live with as much class and dignity and style as they can in the face of this tragic destiny, which is very noble and inspiring. That was the kind of magic that I was interested in. And of all his fiction, *The Sun Also Rises* remains, I think, the most pleasurable for me. I think *A Farewell to Arms* has beautiful and powerful writing about war in it, but the relationship between the two principals is a little bit mannered. His *Moveable Feast* is one of the great memoirs, and shows his style had not abated at all. And I think some of his stories are absolutely wonderful: "Hills Like White Elephants" is an example of absolute virtuosity, a tour de force.

But I think the great thing about Hemingway is that he created an entire mode of morality, a kind of understated, stoical way of being a man and meeting with war in the middle of the twentieth century—as in the well-known phrase "grace under pressure." Much of this moral code of manhood in the service of justice is somewhat spurious, but justified entirely by the quality of the literature with which it's surrounded. And then it went into the movies. Rick in *Casablanca*, Sam Spade in the Dashiell Hammett books, the Raymond Chandler detectives—all of them, I think, owe a great deal to Hemingway and to the kind of courageous, understated, shadowy, anti-fascist hero of few words who went on to loom so large in popular fiction and in Hollywood. *Casablanca,* for example, ostensibly has nothing to do with Hemingway, but it is extremely Hemingwayesque in terms of its aura and its philosophical underpinnings. So in a way, Hemingway was responsible for creating a whole world.

DO: Like Hemingway, Conrad is a novelist with whom critics frequently compare you, particularly vis-à-vis your common interest in the secret menacing forces at work in society and on the psyche. To what extent do you yourself identify with him? And why is *Victory* one of your favorite Conrad novels?

RS: Conrad had a view of history and of human destiny as it was represented in the British imperial system that he knew—a rather Nietzschean view of the world as a brutal place that responds only to strength. And his plots often set out to illustrate that view, and to illustrate the fact that even though the strong rule, there is a degree of futility to that, too—a certain sense that you really can't win, although you have to try. And that's what Conrad's plots, in a way, are about.

Axel Heyst, the main character in *Victory,* is one of the most remarkable characters in English fiction. Conrad sets up the situation in which Heyst is trying to get away from the world, yet finds himself in possession, as it were, of a treasure, and responsible for somebody who has gone to him for protection. Mr. Jones and his sinister assistant set off in pursuit of Heyst and his possessions, and it falls to Heyst to protect himself and to protect those who have come under his care. For me, the novel comes together with its wonderful and terrifying juxtaposition of all these different characters driven by different motivations in pursuit of each other. There is something very classic about this story, and it says a great deal about what Conrad believed about what people end up being required to do in the world, whether they are successful or not. Just in the course of reading it, I discovered how a novel is made—how you take people's desires, their attempts to do right, to do wrong, to get what they want, and you bring them together to make a novel. This struck me as the essence of how to make a plot, because I had always felt there is something kind of second-rate about plot; it is the kind of thing that Conrad himself might have called "higher nonsense." Imitating events and fate is a cheap trick. So you have to try to make plot mean something more than it means itself. You have to make it a metaphor. A plot that doesn't function as metaphor is just a game, and a not very worthwhile game.

DO: It's a technique that's similar to your own, where you introduce each character individually to the reader, and then their lives suddenly start to intersect in ways we never would have anticipated. And the other thing Conrad does, which you do so well, is create a sense of foreboding—a sense that disaster is going to strike, no matter what the characters do.

RS: Yes, yes. I found that really effective in *Victory*. Jones is a terrifying figure.

DO: Like Axel Heyst, Owen Browne, the hero of your novel *Outerbridge Reach*, is also beset by terrifying forces that eventually prove to be too powerful to overcome. After it was published, you said you had come to empathize with him, because you, too, had bitten off more than you could chew in the book. How did you decide to write this book, which is different in many ways from your other novels?

RS: There is something compelling about a man who sets out to do more than he is able to do, because we *all* have to do more than we're able to do—or at least we have to try, in order to get anything done. We have to set out to do what we can, but we also have to aim higher than our ability will allow us, if we want to succeed. Yet anybody who accomplishes something real will sometimes think of him- or herself as a phony—even a person who achieves great things. There is a level on which the real artist, the real achiever, the real saint, will think of himself as a con man, a wrongdoer. I think it's just something in human nature that makes even those who accomplish the greatest good feel guilty.

The Crowhurst story [involving an English sailor who entered a single-handed race around the world and falsified his position] seemed particularly to fit in with this notion. But when I first read the story in the newspaper back in the sixties, I couldn't have sat down and fictionalized it. I had a whole lot of living to do before I could turn that into fiction, and I wasn't going to be ready to write that as a novel until late in the eighties. I had a long, long way to go.

DO: So the feeling of having bitten off more than you could chew came partly from anxiety that not enough time had passed, yet there you were, trying to write the book?

RS: I always feel that. I always feel that I'll never be able to bring this off. I think when you aim high, you always panic. So in that sense there was nothing that made this book different from all the books—it just seemed symbolically more apt.

DO: Speaking of symbols, "The Sufferer," the tiny Mayan carving that the filmmaker Strickland wears around his neck in this novel, reappears in other guises throughout *Outerbridge Reach*. Of course, all of the major characters in your novels are sufferers of one kind or another—I'm thinking in particular of Owen, in this novel, who commits suicide, and Justin, in *A Flag for Sunrise*, who is tortured to death. Why is this kind of agony so much a part of the fictional worlds you create? And what do you have to do to write scenes like these?

RS: I suffer. Writing both those scenes was to me an overwhelming emotional experience. In a way, the death of Owen was more awful to write because it represented a denial of hope and faith, unlike the death of Justin. So yes, writing those was very hard, very hard and risky. But I think it is inevitable in the kind of writing I do now. The victim suffers. The witness, to some extent, suffers. They live in a post-war, existential world, without meaning and without hope.

DO: Do you sometimes wish that you could write something that didn't involve so much personal suffering on your own part, or for your characters?

RS: Well, I think it is time for me to explore style and mode and the possibility of changing in various ways. I think you can work a system to a certain point, and then I think you should see what you can do about employing other modes and methods. I'd like to write something purely humorous. I mean, there's always humor in what

I write—sometimes it's pretty tough humor—but I'd like to write something that was purely funny.

DO: Have you started yet?

RS: I've started but I haven't finished it. I have something in the machine, though, I'd like to write. It would be, I think, pretty hard-edged satire, more for fun, without tragic dimensions. And I've always wanted to write about my childhood, though I'd rather do it as a memoir than, I think, a novel—thought it's going to come out as a fiction anyway. That's inevitable. And there are a couple of novels up my sleeve that I hope to get done before too long.

DO: You mentioned faith a moment ago, and of course that's an issue that figures prominently in all of your novels, as well, most recently in *Damascus Gate*. To what extent do you share your characters' evolving attitudes towards faith and religion?

RS: I think I do share my characters' attitudes. What they believe or what they fail to believe or what they reject are what I believe or fail to believe or reject. They experience the same temptations to faith, the same experiments in faith that I experience; I share their religious dimensions and speculations. In *Damascus Gate* there is much more hope and possibility than in my previous novels. There's an ongoing pilgrimage, an ongoing quest, and the characters are by no means defeated; there are all kinds of possibility for the divine to reveal itself, to manifest itself in various possible ways. Beyond that, it's difficult for me to talk about it right now. I think something is in progress now that I'm trying to deal with; I'm not sure what it is, but I think I have to try and write it out.

DO: What inspired you to travel to Israel, and to the West Bank and Gaza, and to write a novel set in that part of the world?

RS: After I had done a travel piece in Egypt, I left via the Sinai and took a bus from Eilat up to Jerusalem, arriving just at dawn. And I was so taken with Jerusalem that I really wanted to go back. When I did go back I had various introductions to people in the UN and in the journalistic community and in the diplomatic community, and it turned out to be completely my kind of place. And so I went back repeatedly and got together these characters who always turn up in books of mine.

DO: In what sense was Jerusalem your kind of place?

RS: It's a place where you can hear the sound of the world turning. A place where the cosmic, the transcendental, meets the quotidian. Where what ordinary people do has a tremendous spiritual resonance. Where the actions of ordinary people and the actions of what we conceive of as a divine power intersect. And it's also a place where at parties reporters and spies and ideologues are all dining together and falling in love. I mean, it's a place that's hard to beat.

DO: Your sense of place that you create in your novels is something that ordinary writers as well as critics invariably talk about, along with the vast expertise of your characters in areas that most people consider pretty esoteric. How did you go about researching these aspects of *A Flag for Sunrise* and *Outerbridge Reach*?

RS: The way in which I got the background scenes for them was very different. With *A Flag for Sunrise,* I wasn't looking for a novel; it came to me. I had been traveling in Central America—I wanted to look at some of the ruins and do a little diving. It was really a touristic exploration of an area. But I got into conversation with some Americans who were stationed at the embassy in Managua, and I realized that there was a lot going on there that was really very little known in America. So I made another trip that was by way of research, where I was really looking for what was going on, and ended up using Nicaragua in the fictional country called Tecan that I created for the novel. Then I tied this to a story of an individual and his sense of religious and spiritual seeking, his ability to discover what his beliefs were and to be true to them.

As I said before, *Outerbridge Reach* was distantly based on an international, round-the-world race that actually took place in the sixties. The notion of somebody entering a race and faking the result seemed to me to be a metaphor for truth and falsehood so representative of the contemporary world. But in order to write about the two principal technical topics that are in the book—one being sailing, and the other being documentary filmmaking—I had to set out to learn a great deal. Now, I had been at sea a little bit when I was in the navy and when I was in the merchant marine, but I have to emphasize that I was not a knowledgeable sailor at all. At the time, I didn't even own a boat. So in addition to sailing, I had to really go out of my way to make myself acquainted with the boat-brokerage industry and the boat-building industry. I had to learn about the manufacture of boats in the Far East, for example, as opposed to Europe, by finding the right people to question, and by asking the right questions. And also, of course, there was the documentary film aspect to deal with. What is sound? What is the soundtrack on a documentary film? What would happen if you removed the sound from a documentary in those predigital days? All of those things had to be discovered and passed on to the reader with a sense of the world as it was at that time.

DO: I guess, then, you found yourself in the position of Strickland, who says he's a man who's always asking questions.

RS: Exactly. I used that line a couple of times in different places. And that refers to myself and to my work as a writer. If you try to create a world and give that sense of the world to the reader, you're always in the position of the man who's going around asking questions. But lately, I think, I take more liberties. I don't worry so much about the total documentary accuracy anymore; I'm more interested in doing my best to get the *spirit* of a place and a time right, and it's hard to figure how to research that.

DO: So many of your novels focus on political upheavals of one kind or another, and their impact on your characters' sense of themselves and their places in the world. What drives you to explore this particular set of circumstances? And what do you think of the critical proposition that Americans are no longer writing, and are perhaps no longer even capable of writing, political novels?

RS: Well, I'm driven by the period we've just gone through, what some people call the American Imperium or the Cold War. The official philosophy of that foreign policy—basically, resistance to militant communism, to the engaged revolutionary spirit—has caused a great deal of moral compromise in our relationship with Latin America and other regions of the world. And we know from what's emerging now in Central America that there was a great deal of compromise and collaboration with some very bad people—and that in some quarters it's still going on, justified by the Cold War. One of my subjects has always been the United States, and individual Americans finding themselves in compromising positions in order to continue playing the game of the Cold War, and how it affected their lives, whether they carry out policy or observe the carrying out of policy. That, and how the ongoing resistance to what we saw as militant Marxism everywhere affected the lives of the peoples in those countries.

As to the critical proposition that Americans are no longer writing political novels, I disagree. I think my novels are pretty political—a number of them have been flat-out political novels—and I'm an American. A lot of the novels about politics in America *are* superficial "insider" books about Washington, and I don't know what to think of those. But I do think that the novel is not as important in literature as it was forty or fifty years ago—and that the novelist is not the figure that he was fifty years ago. Novelists like Hemingway and Gide and so on were tremendously important cultural figures, but I don't think novelists are important any longer, in the judgment of the cultural world. I don't know why that is, but it does seem to be the case.

DO: I read in *Publishers Weekly* the other day that, like *Dog Soldiers* and *A Hall of Mirrors,* your novel *Children of Light* has been optioned for the movies. As a writer, what is it about Hollywood that has attracted you over the years? And have your experiences working in films changed in any way your approach to dialogue or pacing?

RS: I think Hollywood is fun, as a subject, and the making of movies, although it's a very boring procedure to watch, is fun to write about. The whole movie world is entertaining, and it's also an aspect of America that we shouldn't ignore, because it's a great American industry and it represents part of American culture. I was drawn to it because I do dialogue well, and was recruited for it. But working in films hasn't changed my sense of dialogue because it's not something you learn from life. You might be influenced by movies—and I think, to an extent, every writer of a certain generation in America has been influenced by the form of screenplays— but no experience in real life is likely to make its impact on the kind of prose you write. That's something you learn from reading and from writing, something that operates within the world of the imagination. It's not something that can be imposed from without.

DO: There's a wonderful scene toward the end of *Outerbridge Reach* in which a producer responds to Strickland's most recent documentary by defining for him the law of rape—that even the slightest penetration qualifies as a crime—and by observing that even though the Grecian urn in Keats's "Ode" depicts a rape, the speaker concludes, " 'Beauty is truth, truth beauty,—that is all / Ye know on earth, and all ye need to know.' " Why do you believe that as well? And what responsibilities do you think such a belief confers?

RS: We have to believe that, because it is all we have. What it means is that we live well through insight, we do well through insight, we behave well through insight. By the same token, as a writer you have to serve art truly; you ought never go for the cheap shot. You have always to do the best possible work you can, to make the work as honest and free of cant as you can make it. You have to be the best artist you possibly can be.

BOOKS BY ROBERT STONE
    A Hall of Mirrors
    Dog Soldiers
    A Flag for Sunrise
    Children of Light
    Outerbridge Reach
    Bear and His Daughter
    Damascus Gate

Readers who are interested in learning more about Robert Stone are encouraged to explore some of the books that have shaped his writing life:
    Victory, Joseph Conrad
    The Sun Also Rises, Ernest Hemingway
    The Human Comedy, William Saroyan
    USA, John Dos Passos
    Madame Bovary, Flaubert
    Look Homeward, Angel, Thomas Wolfe
    The Pickwick Papers, Charles Dickens
    Jurgen, James Branch Cabell
    Narcissus and Goldmund, Hermann Hesse

Photo Credits

Page 3, © Patricia Pingree

Page 12, © Joyce Ravid

Page 21, © Nancy Crampton

Page 32, © Inye Wokona, ColorsNW Magazine

Page 43, © Jan Cobb

Page 57, © Frances Levine

Page 69, © Frank Stewart

Page 84, © Nancy Crampton

Page 97, © William B. McCullough

Page 109, © Jane E. Levine

Page 121, © Julius Ozick

Page 132, © Gentl & Hyers/Arts Council, Inc.

Page 145, © Margaretta K. Mitchell

Page 157, © Samantha Loomis Paterson

Page 166, © Michael A. Smith

DISCUSSION GUIDE

What Book Changed Your Life?

1. Are there any books that have influenced more than one of the authors interviewed in *The Book That Changed My Life*? Consider why a certain book or author would influence many people. Are there universal themes or qualities prevalent in these work(s) that speak to more people than others?

2. All of the authors interviewed give a list of several or many books that have changed their lives. Do you think that one book can single-handedly change a person's life?

3. What are some ways in which a fiction book could change someone's life, and how do they compare to ways that a nonfiction book could? Are there more similarities than differences?

4. David McCullough is a historian and a writer. Do the books that have influenced him reflect on his profession or interest in history? Are there any books that have influenced you in your profession?

5. Linda Pastan is a poet. What do the poets she says have influenced her have in common with each other? What do they have in common with her? Do any of the other authors interviewed mention poetry as an influence?

6. Can you see any similarities between the writers being interviewed and the authors on their lists, in terms of their writing style? Their background? Do you find that the authors with whom you can identify, with respect to race, gender, upbringing, etc., have more of an impact on you than others?

7. Grace Paley lists *Mother Goose* as one of the books that changed her life. What are some books that you read as a child? How did

they affect you? Can you say that any of them influenced you to the point that you still think about them today?

8. Think about the criteria that define which books influence your life. Consider things like quality of writing, lyricism, themes, setting, plot, and characterization. Would you be more inclined toward a book that is beautifully written, or toward one that speaks to you thematically?

9. Think about books you've read throughout your life. Is your favorite book now the same as your favorite book five years ago? Ten years ago? Consider the course your life has taken. Do changing themes and events in your life reflect changing tastes in literature and art?

10. Finally, make a list of books that have changed your life. Consider why each one is on your list. Try to narrow it down to one book. How did you come to the conclusions you did?

About the Editor

DIANE OSEN, a freelance writer and editor specializing in the arts, has worked with dozens of National Book Award authors during her fourteen-year-long association with the National Book Foundation. Co-editor of *The Writing Life*, an NBA anthology published by Random House in 1996, she is the author of *Royal Scandals* and the co-author of *Great Interview*.

THE MODERN LIBRARY EDITORIAL BOARD

Maya Angelou

•

Daniel J. Boorstin

•

A. S. Byatt

•

Caleb Carr

•

Christopher Cerf

•

Ron Chernow

•

Shelby Foote

•

Charles Frazier

•

Vartan Gregorian

•

Richard Howard

•

Charles Johnson

•

Jon Krakauer

•

Edmund Morris

•

Joyce Carol Oates

•

Elaine Pagels

•

John Richardson

•

Salman Rushdie

•

Oliver Sacks

•

Arthur M. Schlesinger, Jr.

•

Carolyn See

•

William Styron

•

Gore Vidal

A NOTE ON THE TYPE

The principal text of this Modern Library edition
was set in a digitized version of Janson, a typeface that
dates from about 1690 and was cut by Nicholas Kis,
a Hungarian working in Amsterdam. The original matrices have
survived and are held by the Stempel foundry in Germany.
Hermann Zapf redesigned some of the weights and sizes for
Stempel, basing his revisions on the original design.